THE WAY FORWARD

One Scientist's Adventure in Education Reform

Keith Verner, Ph.D.

Cognitive Learning Institute

The Way Forward : One Scientist's Adventure in Education Reform

For information contact :
Cognitive Learning Institute
Hershey Center for Applied Research
1214 Research Boulevard, Suite1021
Hummelstown, PA 17036

Book and Cover design by Seaton Hart
ISBN: 978-0-692-75706-2

First Edition: July 2016
10 9 8 7 6 5 4 3 2

CONTENTS

The Way Forward

A C K N O W L E D G E M E N T S

MUCH OF THIS SHORT BOOK is biographical in nature. Therefore, many of the people that I would like to acknowledge here, those that were influential in my life and work, will be mentioned in much greater detail in the chapters to follow. I will not simply list them again here, as you will meet them in order.

I would however, like to take this opportunity to thank the founding members of the Cognitive Learning Institute board of directors: Jim Connor, Art Mann, A.R. Smith and Denny Zubler. Without their vision, I would likely not have appreciated the need for capturing the story presented between these covers.

I would also like to thank my editor, Sam Ratner. If this work does not read as dryly as a scientific paper, thank Sam. In addition, Dr. Christine Jurasinski-Sanchez has been an invaluable asset to my work since she rotated in my lab as a first-year graduate student. Her dedication to the cause of excellence in science education over the years has been enormous.

Finally, I thank my wife Mary Beth. Her thoughts and ideas have been important at every step of this adventure.

The Way Forward

I N T R O D U C T I O N

I WAS NINE YEARS OLD when John Glenn became the first American to orbit the Earth. At that precise moment, I developed an insatiable desire to conduct my first science experiment: building and launching my own rocket. The Internet didn't yet exist and the Mercury project hadn't yet made it into our family edition of the *World Book Encyclopedia*, so I was completely in the dark as to how to undertake such a project. Nonetheless, my best friend from across the street and I devoted pretty much the entire summer of 1963 to our dream of model spaceflight.

Gathering Materials

Our first problem was that we were unable to get our hands on petroleum fuel or gunpowder, our first two choices for rocket fuel. Our parents were very clear about gasoline. And gunpowder was hard to come by in any quantity besides a role of caps. The next best choice, perhaps the universal fuel for children under ten, was vinegar and baking soda.

We knew from experience that you could generate enough force to blow the cap off of a milk bottle if you poured baking soda and vinegar into it and quickly put the top on. Achieving flight, we thought, was as simple as directing the force of the reaction toward the ground beneath the rocket. Space travel was right around the corner.

We wanted our rocket to look like the rockets we saw on television. We were convinced that it had to be made out of metal and taper towards its nose like the beautiful NASA Mercury rockets. We also surmised a thing or two about "stages" from TV commentators like Walter Cronkite and Chet Huntley. This, in that time and place, was all that we were going to learn from the adults. We were on our own.

We settled on a construction plan that employed a coffee can at the bottom, seated below a large peach can, then a pureed tomato can atop that, followed by a Campbell's soup can, and finally, at the very top, where John Glenn would sit, a small tomato paste can – the nose cone. Each can had a somewhat smaller diameter than the one directly below it. It looked good. With the labels removed, the cans were bright and shiny. John Glenn was, in our case, a grasshopper. We lined the inside of the nose cone with cotton balls to protect him.

Our propulsion system was, we believed, our finest achievement. Applying our understanding of the "stages" we'd heard about on television, we placed the vinegar in an inverted bottle in an upper stage and the baking soda in a lower stage. Pulling a string that uncapped the vinegar bottle would then release the vinegar, which would run down into the baking soda compartment, beginning the reaction that generated the carbon dioxide gas. When the gas built up enough force, we would have lift off… theoretically.

Failure to Launch

Despite many attempts, the best we were ever able to achieve was to count down from ten, pull the string, hear the chemical reaction taking place as foam bubbled out from around the bottom stage onto our driveway launch pad, and watch as our rocket majestically fell on its side.

Even today I find it amazing that a baking soda and vinegar reaction could generate enough pressure and force to move that pile of cans at all. The total mass of the craft must have been many hundreds of grams, including the mass of the fuel, fuel containers, and John Glenn the grasshopper. Maybe it wasn't our propulsion system that moved the rocket at all; maybe it was a gust of wind. In any case, that was the furthest trip for John Glenn the grasshopper and he survived unscathed. We gave up on rockets that day, following our curiosity to the next challenge.

John Glenn the Astronaut

Many years later, I stood with a good friend outside the locked door of a hearing room in the Dirksen Senate Office Building in Washington, DC. I was there to testify before a Senate Committee on Health, Education, Labor, and Pensions about the reauthorization of the National Science Foundation and the importance of excellent science education for children across the country. After building a career as a research scientist and serving on a school board I was beginning to understand the challenges schools face teaching not just science facts but *scientific thinking*, and I hoped that the committee had brought me to the capitol to talk about what I'd learned. At that moment, though, I just wanted to figure out where I was supposed to go to get into the hearing room.

The rather wide hallway we were standing in was nearly impassable due to a crowd of photographers, reporters, and young men and women that looked uncomfortable in their neckties and business suits. Many of them sat on the floor against walls some distance from the locked door, flipping through papers.

We waited with everyone else, keeping as near the locked door as possible. Even though it was not very hot outside for a June morning in DC, it was getting noticeably stuffy in the hallway. Then we noticed a commotion and movement of bodies in the crowd to the right. Voices raised and cameras flashed. There was laughter and wave of hands. Although the throng of bodies was tight, a gentleman seemed to breeze through it almost unimpeded by the crowd. In his hand he held a leash and was followed by a fairly substantial terrier. He smiled broadly and acknowledged various individuals without stopping or slowing down. He moved through the crowd, passed us, opened and entered a dark wooden door next to the locked hearing room, and was gone.

I turned toward my friend. "That was Ted Kennedy," I said. "And his dog," added my friend. Dr. Michael Poliakoff had recently served as the Deputy Secretary of Education of Pennsylvania for four years and had worked in government and education in some capacity his entire career.

Lacking confidence about where I should be, but guessing it wasn't the hallway, I said goodbye to Michael and followed Kennedy and his canine companion through the unlocked door he had just used. It opened into some sort of waiting room. There was a large desk and rich leather and wood trim throughout. An American flag stood by the desk and the walls were scattered with various framed images and documents. Across the room from the desk were two leather couches facing each other and separated by a low wooden coffee table. On one of the couches sat Senator Kennedy with one leg casually resting across the other knee and his arm stretched along the back of the couch. On the other side of the coffee table sat former Senator and renowned astronaut, John Glenn. They were smiling and talking with each other.

I had known that John Glenn would be testifying in the same hearing, but actually seeing my childhood hero put me into a temporary daze. What could I say to a man who was making huge advances in space travel when I was knocking over cans with baking soda and vinegar in my family's driveway? Luckily, the senators were less starstruck by my presence than I by theirs.

As I walked in, the two men looked up at me for a very brief moment, smiled and then continued talking. Kennedy's dog sat on the carpeted wooden floor next to him. The senator took a green tennis ball from the dog's mouth and tossed it across the room. It thumped into a wall beneath some pictures. The dog scampered off to retrieve the ball and the two senators kept talking. As the door closed behind me, I noticed the relative quiet of the office compared to the crowded hall outside. It was also much cooler. Kennedy turned to me, "Hello," he said "Can we help you?"

"I'm Keith Verner." I said, still standing just inside the door.

"Ah, Dr. Verner. We're all here then," he said as he glanced at a wall clock behind the desk, "Take a seat Dr. Verner. We'll start soon." There were only the two couches as seating options, so I sat next to the astronaut.

After several more tosses of the tennis ball and a friendly discussion between the senators about family and sailing it came time for the hearing to begin. I followed the others through a double door that lead into the hearing room. We walked down a short aisle between neatly aligned rows of wooden chairs into the paneled chamber. Kennedy took his place at the center of a semicircular bench on a raised platform, opening toward and facing the crowd. Ten or so other senators were either seated at the table or mulling around and talking to assistants who would sit behind them once the hearing began. At the foot of the semicircular bench sat dozens of photographers on the floor. They snapped, flashed, and made adjustments. Senator Kennedy's dog sat on the floor directly in front of its master, amidst the horde of photographers.

The three of us witnesses were seated at a long wooden table facing the senators with our backs to the crowd. There were nameplates for each of us in front of our microphones. Through a door behind the right side of the main table, Senator Hillary Clinton appeared and took her seat. I didn't recognize most of the other Senators.

While the legislators got ready and the photographers fiddled with their equipment, periodically taking photos of the senators, I sensed that I had a chance to actually have a conversation with John Glenn. I had so many questions to ask him, but as I opened my mouth the only thing that came out was the story of my childhood attempts to launch the tin can rocket with John Glenn the grasshopper in the tomato paste can nose cone.

When I got to the part where we thought that the baking soda and vinegar reaction might actually have been responsible for knocking the spacecraft over, John Glenn said "Oh really, baking soda and vinegar, then what?" I really didn't want to tell John Glenn, the first American to orbit the Earth, that my failure to launch his grasshopper namesake on my driveway caused me to give up on space travel, but, on the other hand, how could I lie to an American hero? So I thought a moment and told him the truth: "I gave up on rocketry and started studying grasshoppers." He chuckled, and Senator Kennedy called the hearing to order.

The truth is that the decision to study grasshoppers, other living things, and eventually the way the brain works put me on the path to thinking about science education. If I'd stuck with rocketry I might never have found myself in that hearing room, never would have left research science to develop K-12 science curricula, and never would have seen a new approach to science education succeed in classrooms across the country. As is so often the case in science, a failed experiment opened doors to a future I couldn't have imagined.

As it turned out, on that day the senators were uninterested in my thoughts on the importance of scientific thinking. Instead, they asked me and the other witnesses repeatedly about American children lagging behind Chinese and European children in the rote memorization of science facts. They wanted to know why Americans weren't being taught to an internationally agreed upon test. At that point, there was no appetite for a fundamental rethinking of American science education.

Today, years into a national obsession with standardized testing, I believe that tide has turned. Around the country I see huge demand for new materials, approaches, and philosophies for teaching science. This book is an attempt to meet that demand, both by telling my own story as a scientist turned science education reformer and by offering a way forward for those who believe, as I do, that significant improvements are within reach for American science education.

PART ONE

CHAPTER ONE

Growing Up With Science

I CAN'T SAY EXACTLY WHEN I became a scientist.

Many would argue that "scientist" is a professional title. I became a scientist, they might say, when I was hired as a professor at the Penn State College of Medicine, or when I published the first scientific paper from my own lab, or when I received tenure for my scientific work. These were all milestones to be sure, but I know that I was a scientist well before any of this took place.

Others might suggest that science is the work of science students, and that I became a scientist when I began my doctorate in biochemistry at Cornell, or before that as an undergraduate biology major. It's true that I was doing scientific work as a student, but I was definitely a scientist before then.

The Way Forward

I believe that I became a scientist as a very young child. Actually, I think that all children are natural born scientists. The defining characteristic of a scientist is not employment status or college major but engagement in scientific thinking. Scientists are people who experiment, who seek to understand the world around them by forming hypotheses and then rigorously testing those hypotheses. Those experiments need not take place in a lab or result in a journal article, they only need to improve the experimenter's knowledge. By that measure, children are the most prolific scientists in the world. We begin conducting experiments as babies and continue every day until we grow comfortable with our knowledge of the world.

Picture a baby in a highchair. He or she holds a spoon in their small hand, perhaps dangling it over the arm of the highchair. They feel it slip through their fingers and then see it drop through the air and crash to the floor. They look at the spoon on the floor for as long as their very short attention span can manage. Next, an adult or older sibling picks up the spoon and places it back on the tray of the baby's highchair. As soon as they turn away, crash! The spoon is dropped again. The baby looks at the spoon on the floor again and gets excited. Once again the spoon is picked up off the floor for the baby and once again, crash! Next comes Cheerios, a plastic cup, and anything else available to be dropped to the floor, making different noises and eliciting various responses from the adults nearby.

The baby was practicing science. It observed the spoon drop the first time and found it interesting. Through repeated drops, it established a cause and effect relationship that it found was reproducible. Finally, it established that the cause and effect relationship was not a property unique to the spoon, but applied to other objects as well.

These experiments typically end with the baby being

plucked from its seat, wiped off, and put down for a nap. Nonetheless, as the baby sleeps, neurological changes occur in its growing brain. Genes are activated, proteins are produced, and connections between the baby's brain cells begin to rearrange themselves to cement recent events into its permanent memory. This is an ongoing process—a series of broken dishes and scraped knees establishes the concept of gravity well before a child's first science class. Children will never forget the causal relationship between mass and gravity, even though they will never remember their first experiments that proved it.

Great scientific thought arises from the same system of observation and interpretation that drives infant explorations in gravity. Galileo Galilei and Sir Isaac Newton, two of the most prominent contributors to the world of physical science, made observations about the motion of falling objects. Their interpretation of these observations led to the concepts of inertia, gravity, and Newton's Three Laws of Motion. In the biological world, scientists such as Antonie van Leeuwenhoek and Robert Hooke used microscopes to make observations about the structure of plant and animal cells, as well as microorganisms found in saliva. Their observations served as the foundation for understanding cells and cellular structure and eventually for understanding the microbial basis of many diseases.

Young students are not very different from scientists such as Newton and Leeuwenhoek. They possess natural curiosity about the world around them and they continually make observations. However, one difference between young students and professional scientists is that professionals are trained to record their observations in enough detail that others can understand—and even recreate—the experiment after the fact. It is this attention to detail and to labeling that often sets the novice and scientific expert apart.

Therefore, as one of the earliest activities in science instruction, young students should be given multiple opportunities to observe interesting materials and phenomena. Students should then be tasked with describing their observations in as much detail as they are capable of given their mastery of the language. Also, as early as possible, they should be tasked with drawing and labeling their interactions with materials, to build scientific habits.

When children learn science through direct experience, regardless of their age, the effect is much the same as when the baby experiments with a spoon in its highchair. Learning like this creates a deep, almost visceral understanding of the phenomena studied. This type of learning will not soon be forgotten. When we combine experiential learning with the training to record and communicate observations, we turn a child's natural inclination for scientific thought into real scientific skills.

I had a memorable version of this experience myself as I came up as an amateur, and then professional, scientist. As a child, I spent countless warm summer hours watching tadpoles—the aquatic, larval form of frogs—with my friends in shallow Michigan ponds in the woods near my house. I recall first seeing the massive, sticky egg clusters near the pond's edge. One day, nearly all at once, the small, fish-like tadpoles emerged. They swam (more like wiggled) and swarmed by the thousands in the water. They were fun to play with and extremely easy to catch! A single sweep of an open Mason jar would yield a dozen captives.

As time passed, the free-swimming, fish-like tadpoles did something very strange. They sprouted legs! Hind legs first, if I recall, then front legs. After gaining appendages, the tadpoles lost their tails and became frogs, and then could hop out of the water. Thousands of tiny frogs appeared in the mud and grass around the pond.

Perhaps it can be ascribed to the brevity of the childhood attention span, or perhaps it was the beginning of sandlot baseball and other summer activities, but appearance of the frogs always marked the end of my amphibian-watching season. Nonetheless, one question remained on my mind— what happened to the tadpole tails? We searched for, but never found, a single tadpole tail. Where did they go when the tadpoles lost them?

A decade passed. As an eighteen-year-old college freshman, I sat one evening in the library and read an assigned chapter about cellular organelles in a biology textbook. With my yellow highlighter in hand, I learned that small subcellular structures called lysosomes contained dozens of strong digestive enzymes, called hydrolases. The hydrolases could breakdown almost anything they came in contact with. Materials brought into the cell, such as small food particles, would come in contact with the lysosomes and the hydrolases digested the food.

I had a lot of homework to do, and I might have just turned the page and continued my highlighting. However, there was one additional point about lysosomes that the textbook mentioned: lysosomes were thought to be involved in morphogenesis, the process of, among other things, the degradation of tadpole tails. I dropped my highlighter.

Tadpole tails and lysosomal hydrolases, of course! The tails didn't drop off; they were absorbed. The materials that made up the tadpole tails were broken down and reused to make legs… perfect! Somehow, the tadpole tail cells simply knew when it was time for their lysosomes to spill their powerful hydrolases into their own cytoplasm and destroy themselves. Everything seemed to make sense. Biology was wonderful. There was an answer for everything. A great feeling of confidence came over me.

Unfortunately, that wonderful feeling of understanding lasted only a few peaceful moments. How did the lysosomes know they were in tadpole tail cells? How did the lysosomes know it was time and that the tail was no longer needed? What if tadpole brain cell lysosomes mistakenly thought they were in tadpole tail cells instead and dumped their nasty hydrolases into the tadpole's growing brain?

Nothing else I was studying seemed as interesting to me as lysosomes. I read way more about the subject than my courses warranted. I chatted with a fellow biology student I often studied with. What if there was some way to make lysosomes in cancer cells think they were in a tadpole tail cell that was ready to be destroyed? Wouldn't that kill the cancer cells?

We read all we could find. One idea sprang from another. Then we came to a point I had never experienced before. Call it a wall, one that no scientist can ever avoid. That wall represented not just the limit of what we personally knew about the subject of lysosomes, but the limit of what *anyone* knew about the subject at the time! Somehow, my friend and I were confident, controlling lysosomes could cure cancer. But we weren't sure of how. And the details we needed to proceed in our thinking simply did not exist. It seemed so important, but it was out of our hands. The questions we asked could only be answered by new research. We were eighteen-year-old freshmen. We had many other classes to take and pass before we would be in a position to have a lab and write research grants and make new discoveries about lysosomes and cancer on our own. We moved on, disappointed that we hadn't cracked the code to treating cancer but energized by our belief that the answers were out there to be found.

To this day, the potential of controlling lysosome activity in cancer cells is still the subject of research. Although I have left the bench of active research, I continue reading about the topic and cheering for the researchers' success in finding effective cancer treatments.

There is great value in introducing children to scientific concepts and phenomena that they might not be able to fully understand at the time. The introduction serves to pique their imagination and keep their eyes open for answers. At its best, a science curriculum organizes a series of observations and information that can grow with a student as they mature. This way, when an answer finally becomes clear to the student, perhaps months or even years later, it contains depth and meaning that would be impossible to acquire through a brief encounter or a canned explanation.

When we offer children experiences that drive their scientific tendencies, training to build their communication skills, and a glimpse at the breadth, and the limits, of scientific knowledge, we are offering them a future in which they remain as engaged with the world around them as they were as children.

Personally, I always sought to maintain that childish engagement with the natural world. I studied biology in college and, upon graduating, took the first job I could find that would keep me in the orbit of science and scientists. What follows, starting with that job, is the story of my life in science and science education, and of the development of the principles of science education that brought me from watching John Glenn on TV to chatting with him in a congressional hearing room.

C H A P T E R   T W O

First Real Job

WHEN I FIRST GRADUATED from college, my wife Mary Beth and I packed up everything we owned and drove from Michigan to the north Pacific coast. There I had a job in fisheries biology at the National Marine Fisheries Service (NMFS) in the National Oceanic and Atmospheric Administration (NOAA). While the large names and federal designations are impressive in print, the building I arrived at for my first day of work was an old, abandoned Coast Guard rescue station at the mouth of the Columbia River with only a 12 inch diameter NOAA sticker on the front door to tell me I was in the right place.

It was actually a very good location for a Coast Guard station, as the bar of the Columbia River had taken the lives of many seamen over the years. The combined force of the outflowing Columbia River waters slamming into the incoming tide from the Pacific Ocean created surges, currents and waves that were known to swallow entire ships. I would have numerous opportunities to cross the bar on our forty-foot NMFS research vessel, the *Egret*.

The field station chief at the time was a University of Wisconsin-trained fisheries biologist named Terry Durkin. Before coming to the Columbia, he had worked with a huge team to effectively manage the sea lamprey infestation on the Great Lakes. The lampreys--ugly, eel-like, parasitic fish-- are native to the Atlantic Ocean but migrated into the Great Lakes by the 1940s and began to wreak havoc on native fish populations. The biologists who worked to contain the sea lamprey were considered to be heroes in the fisheries field.

Terry could well have been a character in a Hemingway book. He enlisted in the US Navy in 1945 and served as an air traffic controller at Pearl Harbor, Hawaii. Despite his many accomplishments, he was one of the most down to Earth, humble scientists I have met. So humble that it was not until after his death, some twenty years after I left the field station, that I learned in his obituary that he played right tackle for the University of Washington-Madison Badgers in the 1953 Rose Bowl game against the University of Southern California. I can only reflect back on our many discussions about sports on the *Egret* in amazement that he never used any occasion to brag or even mention that he played Big10 football.

My job was to collect benthic samples from the estuary and analyze the invertebrates that I found in the samples. Benthic samples are samples drawn from the bottom muds and sand of the estuary. In a river, the water is constantly moving, and the organisms that live in the flowing water are free to move from one location to another, making them hard to measure. The benthic community of organisms, conversely, was somewhat more stable and predictable from location to location. While I functioned as an aquatic invertebrate biologist, at the field station, the position was simply referred to as a "bug-picker".

The Life of a Bug-Picker

Terry later told me that he hired me because I was trained in Michigan. That was it. Beside one class in limnology--that is, the study of freshwater - I had no experience that formally qualified me to be a federal bug-picker. Fortunately, I was assigned to a true expert aquatic invertebrate biologist and wonderfully well-rounded naturalist, Bob Emmett.

Bob and I shared an office with two desks set up with stereomicroscopes and thousands of little vials of invertebrates preserved in ethanol. To identify the small creatures that we captured in the bottom grab samples, we would put the collected material, ethanol and all, in glass petri dishes and examine it under a stereomicroscope.

We used pure, 200-proof ethanol that was stored in 50-gallon drums in the field station basement, for use both as a preservative and for adding potency to the eggnog during the station's Christmas party. During the hot summer months, the thousands of vials and open petri dishes of ethanol-soaked invertebrate samples that we worked over most of the day would evaporated and release alcohol fumes into the air. We were happy by lunch and tired by the end of the day. Once we realized that we were spending part of the day drunk on ethanol fumes, we built fume-hoods and vented them out the window with fans.

After we'd sorted out our accidental intoxication problem, Bob began in earnest to teach me about the incredible array of life we were there to study. The Columbia River estuary is an enormous body of water running from the Pacific Ocean some 60 miles upriver to the Bonneville Dam – from pure salt water to pure fresh water and everything in between. Thus, when dropping a small sampling grab overboard, one never knew what would come up.

With time I learned to identify some of the organisms in the samples down to the species level. From salt water sampling sites we found marine invertebrates like coral pieces, polychaete worms, small starfish, and juvenile Dungeness crabs. In the freshwater samples we found clams, oligochaete worms, snails, and so on. In between we saw almost everything. Copepods, decapods, and the ubiquitous amphipods. Occasionally we happened upon larval fish. We worked with invertebrate animals from hundreds of taxonomic groups and in various stages of development, which made identifying them all the more difficult. We constantly referred to field keys and books to help with identification. There was no Internet, of course, so we were restricted to the information in our books.

One constant, though, were amphipods. Amphipods--important because of their role as young salmon food--appeared in nearly every sample. They spanned salinity levels. They consumed rotting detritus that appeared throughout the estuary. They were all over; the little ants of the benthic community. Like the ants that scurry around playgrounds and back porches, they had hundreds of different species. Billions of these creatures were crawling in the benthic mud, all looking pretty much the same, and it was my job to tell them apart.

It was during these bug-picking days that I developed a working understanding of the diversity of life. I saw many examples of nearly every phyla of living aquatic organisms.

What is more, by seeing so many closely related groups of animals living together, with body structures similar to but distinct from one another, I could see with my own eyes the evolutionary relationships that existed between them. In addition, by microscopically studying body structures such as gills, appendages, and mouthparts in relation to the physical characteristics of the sample sites, I was able to see how animals had adapted to their environment. It was a practical education that I would cherish my entire subsequent career.

Perhaps the greatest satisfaction of my time as a bug-picker was when I identified a rare freshwater polychaete worm, *Manayunkia Speciosa*. Polychaete worms almost universally live in saltwater, with very few exceptions. Yet that is where we found our worm, in freshwater. To be sure of my identification I wrote a letter and sent a sample to the Smithsonian Institution. In a return letter, my identification was confirmed and represented an extension of the known range of this organism in North America. The sample was numbered, cataloged and entered into the Smithsonian collection. I was encouraged to write a short paper on where we found *M. Speciosa*, which was later published in a small, very slightly read journal. Despite a number of subsequent scientific articles, all in much more widely circulated journals, *Two Sabellid Polychaetes of the Columbia River Estuary* was my first and favorite. Perhaps it was because I wrote it on a notepad in an old Coast Guard station on a spectacular river with just a hint of ethanol vapor in the air!

Mount Saint Helens

During sampling, I spent a considerable amount of time on the *Egret* with Bob, Terry, and a number of other biologists and fishermen. We would sample for several days at dozens of stations all over the estuary every month of the year. One of the things I loved about the estuary was the feeling of its permanence. It was vast, and its natural rhythms dictated our lives within it. Tides were predictable each day. Juvenile salmon ran downstream after growing to fingerlings in the tributaries where they hatched, and adult salmon ran back upstream after growing to enormous size feeding in the ocean for a few years. Commercial fishermen waited for them and the fish arrived each year like clockwork. These things were constant. In fact, except for the number of fish, Lewis and Clark saw the same things we did when they reached the estuary in the first decade of the nineteenth century.

On clear days, we saw the 9,677 ft. snowcapped profile of Mt. Saint Helens from the *Egret*. It loomed before us, another symbol of ancient stability, maybe even more potent than the estuary itself. From our distance we could see the snow cap increase and recede with the change of the seasons. Mt. Saint Helens has stood there for some 50 million years.

One of the most distinctive characteristics of Mt. Saint Helens was its smooth, conical peak – considerably different from the more jagged peaks of Mt. Hood and Mt. Rainer, for example. If one can have a "favorite" mountain, then I would say Mt. Saint Helens was mine for this reason – its almost perfect, graceful, smooth symmetry. I recall standing on the *Egret* on a Friday, looking at Saint Helens and thinking that some things last forever.

Two days later, on Sunday, May 18, at 8:32 in the morning, Mt. Saint Helens erupted. An enormous blast hurled pulverized rock down the side of the mountain at speeds approaching 670 mph. Mt. Saint Helens dropped from

9,677 ft. to 8,365 ft. in elevation, changing from a perfectly smooth cone to a jagged peak. A crater two and a half miles wide and over 2,000 feet deep replaced the symmetrical cone within a period of 10 seconds.

As the eruption continued, gas, mud, rock, and debris, collectively known as pyroclastic flow, rushed down the side of the mountain at speeds up to 155 mph. The flow destroyed trees and covered highways as far as 19 miles away, and filled in lakes and river valleys with up to 600 feet of mud. Fifty-seven people lost their lives in the eruption.

The flow of material down river valleys eventually reached the Columbia River, dumping enormous amounts of mud and felled trees that would then head downstream to the estuary, where we were, about 70 miles from the blast. Early the next morning, we boarded the *Egret* for a 36-hour, non-stop trip to collect fish and benthic samples. We all knew this was likely a once in a lifetime chance to directly observe the immediate impact of a volcanic eruption on a commercial fishery.

It is difficult to forget the sound of the many felled trees from Mt. Saint Helens that floated through the estuary banging into the side of the *Egret* as we worked aboard in the dark. I recall looking over the gunnel into the dark water and seeing bright white, baseball-sized objects floating by. Grabbing one, I found that it was a floating rock from the volcano, a pumice stone. We saw them on the river for several weeks afterward.

We learned many scientific lessons from our Columbia River estuary studies in May of 1980. Over the years, however, the one thing that "sticks" more than any single detail is the absolute certainty of enormous and awesome change on Earth. With time, forests can evolve into desserts. Lakes can fill in and become grasslands. Given enough time, continents drift over the surface of our planet like pumice stones over the water. If an entire mountain could be so radically transformed before our very eyes, then nothing is permanent.

An Environmentalist

The Army Corps of Engineers funded most of the work we did at NMFS. This was because the Corps was responsible for maintaining a shipping channel through the estuary and river for commercial and naval navigation. Each year, the Columbia River carries countless metric tons of silt and sediment from the mountains and valleys it drains. This results in a sediment plume that extends well into the Pacific Ocean and can easily be seen from space. This same silt and sediment also acts to constantly refill the river's navigation channels. When enough sediment accumulates, the channels become too shallow and navigation becomes dangerous. Thus, on a continual basis, the Corps has to dredge the channels.

Dredging requires the Corps to remove the sediment from the navigation channels and put it somewhere else. The problem from an environmental perspective is where to put all those tons of dredge "spoil." Dumping the spoil somewhere commercially valuable fish, such as salmon, use as a nursery for their fry is a bad idea. Dumping it somewhere with comparatively less biological importance and a rapid current that will wash the spoil out to sea, doing minimal damage to the ecosystem, is far preferable.

One particularly bad place to put dredge spoil is in shallow bays and tidal flats, because these areas nearly always support a great range of life and are ecologically quite important. However, it is precisely these locations that land developers prefer to fill with spoil, because they want to build condominiums and other structures atop the spoil that will have a nice view of the water.

Our responsibility was to study the data we collected and recommend to the Corps of Engineers where it would be least damaging to dump their dredge spoil. We presented our recommendations to the Corps in the form of a report called an *Environmental Impact Statement*. Ultimately, and perhaps unfortunately, the final decision on where dredge spoil would be dumped did not rest with us. Our recommendations were considered along with other information in deciding what to do with the spoil.

I was not born a naturalist and, compared to Bob Emmitt and most of the others at the field station, I wasn't even a very good naturalist. But it is difficult for anyone working in a natural environment that countless species of life depend upon not to become attached and develop a moral obligation to protect it if at all possible.

My days on the Columbia River estuary taught me at a very early age that you could deeply care for what you did in your career on a daily basis. My colleagues there taught me that it was unnecessary to take jobs only for a paycheck – you could get paid for doing what you believed in if you were persistent. I would find this same kind of passion in myself later in my career when it came to the commitment to restructuring and improving science education.

Hands-On Learning

While my study of K-12 science was still a long way off, I learned at NMFS a significant component of the underlying structure of my future work in science education. Everything I learned about fisheries biology, I learned "hands-on." With nothing more than a good teacher and coach in Bob Emmett and a couple of standard identification keys, I acquired a working knowledge of fisheries biology.

I learned about tides by getting our skiff stuck on a sandbar and having to wait hours for the next tide to float us off so that we could go home. I learned about evolution by examining the slight differences in structure of related species compared to the perfect match in structure of individuals of the same species.

I learned that creatures are adapted for life in very specific environments. Some live on sandy bottoms while others live in mud. Freshwater organisms cannot live in salt water, while marine creatures, stopped by an invisible wall of decreased salinity, cannot enter the freshwater tributaries under any circumstance.

By being tossed around on the *Egret* amidst the lines, nets, specimen bottles, wind, and cold, I learned the relevant science much faster than I would have sitting in a library reading the very best books about fisheries biology available. Not only was my hands-on course of study quicker, but also it produced in me a qualitatively different form of knowledge than I could gain from reading. It was a much more visceral, instinctual understanding of aquatic life and its evolution than any number of library hours could have given me. Thus, within a very short period of time I was capable of recognizing and understanding the significance of a polychaete worm in a freshwater sample. Within a year of daily hands-on experience, I went from a college freshman's concept of aquatic biology to contributing a specimen to the Smithsonian Institution, extending the known geographic distribution of a species.

This is the power of "hands-on" learning. Much later I would study the neurobiological underpinnings of hands-on science education. I would apply it to university outreach programs and a national science education curriculum and learning system. But the foundational belief in this system was only reasonable to me because the power of this pedagogical approach was demonstrated to me directly in my own life, through my own senses.

Moving On

The biggest milestone (excluding perhaps the eruption of Mount Saint Helens!) that took place while at NMFS was the birth of my son, Keith. What an event that was. There were no babies in the extended NMFS family at the time. Many of the senior employees had children (including Terry and Ramona Durkins' remarkable brood of eleven), but ten-year olds were the "babies" in the group until Mary Beth became pregnant.

My son Keith turned out to be a sensation. No child had been born within the general confines of the Coast Guard station for some time. His baby shower was held in a lighthouse on the south shore of the Columbia River in Astoria, Oregon. All of our employees were there along with their families. The captain of the *Egret*, a rugged fisherman from Ketchikan, Alaska named Nick, gave us a two-month's supply Gerber's baby food and a lamp for Keith's nursery that played "Jack and Jill" as a little figure rocked back and forth in a chair in time to the music.

By the time Keith was just over a year old, our family – now the three of us - headed to Ithaca, New York, to enter a Ph.D. program at Cornell University. I would never be a practicing environmental scientist again. I would never regret having been one. The years at the NMFS field station were some of the happiest in my life. Among other things, my time there taught me that I could make a living doing science. As I collected tadpoles and built rockets as a child in Michigan, I had no idea that I could actually get paid for doing such interesting things! My NMFS experience showed me that I could follow my interests in science and make a living doing so. Never again would I work in a field in which I was not intellectually invested. Never again would I doubt that science was both a noble *and* a realistic calling. I developed a pride in my work. I developed confidence in myself. Following a scientific process, taking a scientific approach would become second nature to me for the rest of my life.

CHAPTER   THREE

Cornell

MY THESIS ADVISOR AT Cornell was Dr. Tony Bretscher. Tony was trained at Cambridge and Leeds Universities and then did his postdoctoral fellowship in Germany with Klaus Weber. I was Tony's first graduate student and he was not much older than I. Pedigrees are important in scientific training. There are attitudes and perspectives that are passed from thesis advisor to student that are hard to precisely define. At the Ph.D. level, training goes well beyond textbooks and coursework. One works at the limit of what is known and looks over that edge all the time. In such an environment, personal taste and philosophical bent are much more important than an outsider might imagine. Although the experiments are strictly defined and precisely executed, the choice of experiments to attempt, the questions to ask and the interpretation of findings are influenced significantly by one's training. It is at this level that the lineage of scientific training comes into play.

It is difficult to track the development of one's personal and professional character as it is being shaped, but in retrospect my time in the Bretscher lab was formative. I think that because Tony was so close to my own age that it was difficult for me to appreciate all of his qualities at the time. Nonetheless, his ability to lead me in the right direction while I thought such direction was entirely my own design was a skill of his that I only much later would appreciate.

In the early 1980s, the fusion of numerous techniques such as cell fractionation, specific antibody production, fluorescence and electron microscopy caused an explosion in the understanding of cells. There were underlying structures in cells that had never been seen before and yet were responsible for some of the most essential functions of life, from cell division and motility to muscle contraction, transmission of messages along neurons, and a whole host of other fundamental functions. These formerly invisible structures consisted of an entire spectrum of protein molecules and were collectively referred to as the cell's *cytoskeleton*. The cytoskeleton was responsible for both the underlying structure and the whipping motion of the flagella of sperm cells. It performed a similar function in producing cilia on the surface of cells lining our trachea, with coordinated upward beating motions that prevented us from quickly drowning in our own respiratory secretions. It provided the rigidity of surface structures of cells found in our ears, known as stereocilia, that caused them to vibrate at specific frequencies of sound and permitted us to hear.

I was interested in determining how the cytoskeleton was attached to the cell membrane. The membrane that surrounds cells is a thin but complex layer of fat-like materials called lipids. Cells are essentially little sacks of lipid membrane, and without any underlying cytoskeletal support would exist as blobs with little to no structure. Most would form simple spheres. The cytoskeleton pushes and pulls on the cell membrane from inside, and it is through this protein framework that cell structure is derived. Clearly, to have such an effect on the cell membrane, the cytoskeleton must attach to it in some way. For example, if one thinks of the biconcave shape of human red blood cells one may suspect that something must be pulling on the inside of the concave surfaces to maintain this distinctive cell shape. This pull is caused by the cytoskeleton. In fact, mutations in human cytoskeletal proteins are responsible for a disorder called familial spherocytosis. Red blood cells in such individuals lose their typical biconcave structure and form spheres. These cells become easily damaged when passing through small capillaries and are destroyed in the process, particularly in the massive capillary beds of the spleen. In short, cytoskeletons and their interaction with cell membranes are really important!

This is what I was studying and to me it was endlessly fascinating. There was hardly a need to think about anything else. I could become so deeply lost in thought about molecules and cells that getting on the correct bus to go home or paying our rent on time could sometimes become mere interference. This kind of focus on science to the exclusion of real world concerns is endemic to research scientists, some more so than others. I recall one day speaking to an elderly faculty member who worked on fat, or adipose, cells. She was a brilliant scientist and very likeable. About five minutes into the conversation I noticed that she had her dress on inside out.

I think it was Tony's sense of humility and common sense that helped train me to keep at least one foot on the ground while still thinking deeply and scientifically. While I was still at Cornell he married one of the graduate students, a very bright woman named Janice, and they went on to have a wonderful life together while still making continuous scientific contributions. This sense and model of normalcy, priority and balance were much more important to my long-term development than I could ever have guessed at the time. In fact, had I not been able to look beyond the lab bench, to hear the call of social needs in the educational community, I never would have considered becoming a science education advocate and reformer later in my career. Perhaps I'd be wearing my jeans inside out today!

Our second child was delivered at Ithaca Hospital in 1982. Emily was born the night before my Bioenergetics mid-term exam. Mary Beth and I were up all night and Emily came in the very early morning. A couple of hours later Dr. Peter Hinkle handed me the exam. News of Emily's birth had spread quickly through the small Biochemistry network and I recall Peter saying as he held the exam out to me, "You know you don't have to do this now." I took the exam anyway, and did well enough even though I was rushing to return to the hospital.

Students and postdocs got together rather frequently to socialize, often at fairly late hours. One thing we all had in common was that we were poor--I received a stipend from the Biochemistry department of $7,000 per year. We had to entertain ourselves and, given our single-minded obsession with our chosen field, that often meant creating opportunities for scientific observation outside the lab. I recall having eight or nine grad students and postdocs at our home in student housing one evening. We were drinking cans of beer, labeled simply "Beer," and sitting in a circle on the brown carpeted floor in the living room. Very few grad students were married; none had children. Keith was asleep in the bedroom and Emily, an infant at the time, had woken up due to our talking. We laid her down on the carpet in the middle of our circle where she became the topic of conversation and scientific speculation for what may have been hours. Emily's muscle contractions and tone, balance and strength, fat composition, respiratory and pulse rate and energy metabolism all were under significant scientific scrutiny. When she fell back to sleep we lowered our voices and wondered what a one-month old might dream about. We watched closely for rapid eye movements.

"OK, that's enough," Mary Beth said, and we put Emily back in her crib – our evening's entertainment concluded.

Early Thoughts on Science Education at Cornell

Where my interest and eventual commitment to science education began is difficult to say, but I had some opportunities while at Cornell to look up from the lab bench and see the broader questions of learning and teaching that would later shape my career.

It started with my own children. While at Cornell, Keith entered Kindergarten. His first day of school was also the first day of Kindergarten for close to two dozen other five-year olds at Cornell graduate housing where we lived. Hasbrouck housing was composed almost entirely of married students, over half of them foreign, from essentially every country one can think of. In our building alone, we were one of only two American families. The other units housed student families from Guatemala, Trinidad, Korea, Venezuela, and Sudan. Our weekly potluck barbecues in the summer were amazing!

When the bus arrived on the first day of school, a bus that would be entirely filled by Hasbrouck elementary school students, the tears started flowing. Regardless of country of origin, a child's first day of school is monumental. Keith waited for the bus wearing sneakers, blue jeans, and a Michigan State tee shirt and carrying a small knapsack – still a vivid memory. When the bus finally took our children away, the parents looked at each other, wiping their eyes, as if to say, "So what do we do now?"

After my first year, when I had finished essentially all of my coursework and was devoted entirely to my thesis research, my schedule became quite flexible and I was able to devote some time to volunteering at Keith's school. The Kindergarten class was going on a field trip to a local state park to learn about how early European settlers in the area lived. There were a number of small log cabins and the students moved from one cabin to the next in small groups to learn different aspects of pioneer life. I was stationed at one of the cabins and assigned to make butter with the students as they arrived.

To make butter, I used a Mason jar containing a wooden clothespin. The jar was big enough that when I shook it, the clothespin bounced around inside like a rattle. We added cream to the jar and began shaking it. I had the students pass the jar around, as their arms grew tired after about only thirty seconds of shaking. I shook the jar harder and longer when it was my turn, in order to move the process along. It turns out modern Kindergarteners make poor pioneers.

As time passed, everyone noticed that the cream changed its appearance. We opened the jar and removed the clothespin to find it covered in a thick coat of solid, pale yellow butter.

"Why does the butter form on the clothespin?" one of the children asked.

That sounded like a simple question, but when I went to answer I found myself practically drowning in scientific minutiae. The answer had to do with milk fat, which exists in a suspension of droplets in what is called micelles. It also has to do with the hydrophobicity of lipids in an aqueous solution and... What an excellent question.

I was struck by the short distance between a young child's question and the work of what I thought of at the time as "real scientists." Fumbling, I answered as best I could, but fortunately all of the students were distracted by the fact that we were going to spread our freshly churned butter onto slices of bread and eat it for a snack.

Missed Opportunity

I missed another opportunity to think about precollege science education while at Cornell because of my preference for "real science." While living at Hasbrouck I met grad students from every conceivable area of study. Our Sudanese neighbor studied nutritional aspects of beef (Cornell has an exceptional Food Science department and vet school) while our Guatemalan neighbor studied disease resistance in bean crops. We had law students, a number of veterinary students, and our immediate neighbor to the right was getting a Ph.D. in Sociology. There were writers, political scientists, chemists, and so on, all thrown together for several years in a small community in the middle of upstate New York where we ate together, drank together, struggled with our advisors together, and watched our children go off to school for the first time together.

Eventually, I met someone from the College of Education. While I forget his name, I believe he was one of the American students. He was working on a Ph.D. in "science education."

We only met in passing and I never spoke with him again, but in retrospect I must apologize to him for the biased and uninformed attitude that I copped about him after our one and only brief talk. He wanted to understand how young children learn science. As a student in a fairly prestigious "serious" science like Biochemistry, I could not comprehend the challenges of his specialization, which was quite innovative at the time. Instead, I looked down on the "simple" science content taught in grammar school. How could anyone devote so much effort to concentrating on such a trivial pursuit? I had no idea at that time of the study of learning theory, educational psychology, sociology, and political awareness that is ultimately needed to be an excellent science educator. Further, and much worse, I had little appreciation for the fact that he was in a somewhat pioneering field at the time. Today I can say that he was ahead of his time.

Had I been more mature, or perhaps simply less pretentious, I could have learned a great deal about science education at a formative juncture in my own fledgling career. However, I lost that chance through my own ignorance and will always regret it. All that I may have gained from the experience is the habit, developed only much later in life, of finding almost any career or calling interesting if pursued by someone committed to a vision. Perhaps that was enough.

Carl Sagan

The *Public Broadcasting Service* series *Cosmos: A Personal Voyage* written and hosted by Dr. Carl Sagan first aired in 1980. It consisted of thirteen episodes, viewed by a riveted audience across the world. Estimates suggest that some 500 million viewers have watched the *Cosmos* series. I was one of them.

In addition to being a watershed event in the history of science-themed television programming, it made Carl Sagan a household name and spokesman for modern science. He was a familiar guest on television talk shows. He appeared often on the late night *Johnny Carson Show*, where his humor, wit, and charm made him a favorite. Sagan wrote many best sellers based on scientific themes, from the companion book to the *Cosmos* series to the novel *Contact*, about discovering extraterrestrial life.

Sagan was also a professor at Cornell. While I never took a class from him, one of the other grad students in the Bretscher lab did. It was a small seminar class that occasionally met at Sagan's house. I regret not having taken it as well.

When I was in Ithaca, Sagan was rarely there. His public appearances, his work with NASA, and his advocacy against nuclear weapons kept him traveling almost constantly. One evening, however, Sagan gave an open lecture for students on campus, unrelated to any particular course. I went with a Hasbrouck neighbor named Bob Henning, a sociology Ph.D. candidate. Sagan's slides were absolutely incredible. Some of the spectacular images of Jupiter's moons that he got at NASA had not even been made public yet. He pointed out a gorge on one of the moons and told us that he had named it "Ithaca," which brought resounding cheers from the audience. While I had brought my copy of *Cosmos* with me to the lecture, I was too shy to go up afterwards to ask him to sign it. Fortunately Bob had no such inhibition and went up to the stage with my book immediately after the talk ended. He was joined by dozens more students eager to have their copies signed as well. The book still sits in my own small library.

While many of my own professors at Cornell referred to Sagan as a "showboat", the students loved him. After all, he associated the name of our school to the most cutting edge science at the time. He popularized science and was largely responsible for encouraging public support for scientific inquiry and research. I don't know about being a showboat, but Carl Sagan was surely a showman. I always felt that was something to be admired.

In retrospect, there is no doubt that Carl Sagan had a profound impact on my later obsession and dedication to science education. Along with Jonathan Miller's series *The Body in Question*, which first aired in 1979, and David Attenborough's series *Life on Earth*, also first broadcast that same year, *Cosmos* forced me to consider and respect the work and talent required to teach scientific concepts to a lay audience. The influence this had on my future science education work was enormous. However, all that would not occur for a number of years to come.

Efraim Racker

In addition to Tony Bretscher, another professor who had a major influence in my life was Dr. Efraim Racker. As Tony and I began to suspect that the energy-containing molecule ATP might be important in the interaction of cytoskeletal proteins with each other, I sought out the various students and postdocs in the Racker lab who were the real ATP experts. Racker was a very famous European physician and scientist who fled Nazi Germany in the 1930s. He was hugely important in energy metabolism in cells and his work was fundamental in our understanding of how mitochondria produce energy and how energy in the form of ATP is made, stored, and used in cells.

Even before meeting Racker personally, I knew of him because of the notorious "Racker Seminars." This was a graduate student seminar series in which each week a different grad student would present his or her progress on their thesis research. These presentations remain one of the most traumatic events of my life. I would bet the same could be said for each and every other graduate student in Biochemistry. One's Racker date was as significant as Christmas or New Years; certainly more than a birthday or any paper and pencil exam. Even our Ph.D. qualifying exam and final oral exams seemed incidental compared to our Racker talks. Students were brought to tears as Dr. Racker prodded, probed, and criticized – all in front of the entire group of one's peers. No student was allowed to miss the Racker seminars. Therefore, when you died, you died in front of all of your colleagues, all of them.

As first year students we needed only to attend the Racker seminars. We did not present because we had not developed our thesis work to the point of having anything to say based on our own experiments. It was nonetheless terrifying; we saw advanced graduate students, those with published papers, our idols as well as friends, reduced to babbling idiots who left the stage wondering why they wanted to be a doctor in the first place. We met afterwards at Johnny's bar to console the speaker who, after a few beers, would begin to regain use of their legs and cheer up – mainly because it was a full year until their next Racker seminar.

I met Efraim Racker in person a quarter to midnight on a weekday night. The department autoclave--a pressure steamer used to sterilize lab equipment--was located down the hall from the Racker lab in the basement of Wing Hall. It was late but I needed to sterilize some materials for use in an experiment the following morning. When I got to the autoclave, I discovered that one of the ten bars that locked the two-inch thick stainless steel door shut during operation was lying on the floor. I had no idea how to repair it but wanted to go home and figured there were another nine bars to hold the door shut during a short run. I set the machine at 30 psi for 15 minutes at 275°F and threw the switch on. I then ran up to our lab to get a couple of other things ready with a timer for the autoclave in my pocket.

When the elevator door opened on my return to the basement, I heard a hideous, high-pitched scream and the sound of violently escaping gas. I ran down the hall to the autoclave room and turned the corner to find Dr. Racker and his assistant Mike standing by the hissing autoclave.

"Did you do this?" said Racker. The first words he ever spoke to me.

I couldn't answer and didn't need to. Mike, who I always thought had a Charles Manson look about him with his greying beard and long hair, bellowed curses at me for my negligence. I looked back at Dr. Racker. He simply nodded in agreement with Mike.

Time passed. Racker seminars came and went and I survived. Nothing was said of the autoclave incident again. We were on the third floor and Racker's lab was in the basement, so I rarely saw him. It was in my third year that I needed help from his lab on an ATP question and Tony encouraged me to go wherever my questions took me.

One thing led to another and I soon made friends with a visiting Russian postdoc named Sergei and several graduate students who worked with Racker. They told me that while Racker thought of the autoclave incident was a bit careless on my part, he was more impressed that I was there at midnight doing science… as he was, in his seventies. He had a habit, they said, of standing near the outside door at about 5:15pm reading a scientific publication. To leave the building and go home you had to walk by him.

Once, Racker approached me as I headed out of one of his labs after discussing a few matters with people in his group. "Do you have a moment?" he said as he motioned to his office door. I went in. Before I sat down I quickly scanned the many photos on the walls. I counted pictures of Racker with three different presidents of the United States before he motioned for me to sit.

"I've noticed that you have be taking a fair amount of my postdoc's time lately. Is it important?"

I thought it was, and I took the opportunity to explain the main thrust of my investigation into ATP. Sitting in Dr. Racker's office and making the case for my work in great detail, one on one with a scientist I admired was marvelous. Once I heard him say, "that makes sense" for the first time, I could not be stopped until he cut in to tell me that I should nonetheless be prudent with his postdoc's time. He then asked if I'd like to attend his lab's group meetings that were held each Saturday morning. I never missed one of these meetings until I graduated

Those Saturday morning group meetings were awesome. About half the time there would be a presentation by one of Racker's postdocs or visiting professors sharing their recent research results. Being asked to present was a signal to everyone that the presenter's work was the hottest thing going at that time. The rest of the Saturdays, Racker invited famous scientists he knew from all over the globe to visit with us. People I read about in my undergrad textbooks sat across a small conference table from me; people who invented the machinery or discovered the molecules I used in my own research chatted with me while eating lunch from a paper bag packed at Racker's house.

In addition to the cutting edge science, I thoroughly enjoyed hearing stories of long past discoveries and scientists. At that time there was a lot of work going on involving transforming growth factors, molecules that could cause cancer cells to start dividing. Various "TGFs" were being discovered and reported in labs around the world and there was great competition to find and name new ones. At one point, one of our Saturday visiting scientists said, "Be careful. Some of these new TGFs may simply be one of the originals that are contaminated with something else or a mix of two previously known TGFs not completely separated from each other. It could be like the vitamin story."

Us younger scientists looked at each other. "The vitamin story?" one postdoc finally asked.

"Yes, take the B vitamins. We named them as we found them. What do we have now, vitamin B1, B2, B3, B5, B6, B7, B9 and B12? Why do you think we numbered them like that? Where's B4? Or B10, or the others?"

"They were one of the other complexes contaminated with something else!" someone exclaimed.

The older scientists brought this kind of history to the table every Saturday and I was constantly amazed at how much understanding the historical development of research science could help all of us on the more cutting edge projects we worked on.

It was at one of these Saturday morning Racker group meetings that I met my future postdoctoral advisor, Dr. Gottfried Schatz. Gottfried Schatz, who went by "Jeff" in English, was formerly a postdoc in Racker's lab and then went on to receive a professorship in the Cornell Biochemistry department. He worked on mitochondria, as did many other Racker postdocs throughout the years. When I met Jeff, his lab in Basel, Switzerland was studying how internal organelles like mitochondria are constructed. This was called mitochondrial biogenesis and was a very hot field at the time. It was part of a larger question of how the cell makes all of its internal components.

I began reading about mitochondrial biogenesis, and found a remarkable accomplishment from Dr. Schatz's lab. He had eight back-to-back scientific papers published in a single issue of one of the world's most distinguished scientific journals, *The Journal of Biological Chemistry*. Getting one paper into *JBC* was an accomplishment. Having eight back-to-back papers, occupying nearly a quarter of an issue, was unheard of. In retrospect, I am sure that there was some showmanship involved in the feat--the papers could easily have been spread over several issues--but it was a staggering accomplishment nonetheless. Among other things, the glamour of eight back-to-back papers seduced the best graduate students from around the world to apply to the Schatz lab to do postdocs.

I approached Dr. Racker when it was time for me to start considering where I would go for my postdoctoral training. There was no question in my mind that I wanted to work with Schatz. None. Sitting in the same seat that I did the first time I was in his office, I asked for his help. "Ef," I said, addressing him by the nickname the more advanced students and all of his friends used, "I wonder if you think that I could work in Dr. Schatz's lab."

Racker leaned back in his seat. "Well, you know, I've known Jeff since he was your age. It might not surprise you that in my opinion he has one of the best labs in the entire world." He quietly stared at me for a while.

"Would you write a recommendation for me?" I asked.

He smiled. "I'll call him."

Today, long after his death, Efraim Racker is still known for the memorable quips that peppered his books and other writings. Reflecting on my initial meeting with Efraim Racker at a quarter to midnight at the basement autoclave in Wing Hall, being cursed out by his associate Mike for running the broken instrument, I am reminded of one of his quotes that meant little to me years ago when I first read it:

"It doesn't matter if you fall down, as long as you pick something up from the floor when you get up" - Efraim Racker

C H A P T E R   F O U R

Basel, Switzerland

ONE OF MY FIRST FRIENDS in the Schatz lab was a
Dutch postdoc by the name of Dr. Adolphus P. G. M. van
Loon. In addition to his native Dutch, Dolph spoke
excellent German and his English was very good as well,
although he would occasionally have to pause and search
for a word. He showed me around the lab on my first
morning. The Schatz group occupied about half of the fifth
floor of the University of Basel Biozentrum. There were six
or seven labs with a half dozen doctoral students or
postdocs at benches in each. It was a very large operation.
Down one of the halls the stock chemicals were arranged in
cabinets alphabetically from one end of the hall to the other.
It was here that I learned to find *NaOH* and other sodium-
containing chemicals about halfway down the hall in the N's
for *natrium* and potassium with the K's where it belonged.

At some point in the late morning during our tour of the department, I asked Dolph were the restroom was. He seemed puzzled. "The restroom?"

"Yes," I repeated. "The restroom."

Dolph thought a moment. "Well," he said, "we don't do that here."

"What, you're kidding right?"

"No, not at all," said Dolph. "We do that at home. We work here."

"You go home to pee?" I asked in amazement.

"Oh, oh, I see, I see," Dolph laughed, "you mean the water closet. That's down the hall there."

The Schatz Lab

I worked at a bench across from a German postdoc by the name of Dr. Ed Hurt. Ed was one of Schatz's most prolific postdocs at the time. His wife, Geta, worked as a tech in the lab as well. I recall working at my bench and listening to Ed repeat my name over and over to practice his English. It turns out that saying my first and last name is a bit of a problem for German speakers. The "th" in Keith has no equivalent in German. The "h" in the "th" sound gets dropped and my first name becomes "Keit." To a German-speaker, my last name should start with an "f" sound rather than a "v" sound, as "v" is typically the pronunciation of the German "w." Wagner, for example, is pronounced "Vagner." So "Keith Verner" was a problem for even an excellent English speaker such as Ed.

I originally wished to spend my time in Basel working on some aspect of the cytoskeleton, as I had at Cornell. I was interested in the observation that mitochondria and other membrane-bound organelles and vessels are transported the length of nerve cells (neurons) by hitching a ride on cytoskeletal structures. This spread energy production by mitochondria throughout the entire neuron and allowed for the delivery of neuropeptides from the main part of the cell where they were made to the terminus of the neuron, called the synapse. The released neuropeptides would then bind to the neuron on the other side of the synapse and the nerve signal would thus be transferred from one neuron to the next along a pathway of neurons in the system.

However, after some initial experiments, I realized that to get the most out of my experience at the Schatz lab I should probably focus on something more closely related to the work of the other postdocs and graduate students. Therefore, I turned my attention to mitochondrial biogenesis, the targeting and import of proteins into mitochondria.

Without going into great detail, I began experiments to investigate the nature of the reported interaction between cytosolic ribosomes and the mitochondrial surface. Ribosomes are tiny cellular structures, large molecular particles really, that make the cell's proteins. Their association with the surface of mitochondria or any other membrane could suggest that proteins for the organelle to which they are attached are inserted through the membrane to which they are bound.

I loved this work because it involved gene splicing and transcription, *in vitro* synthesis of proteins, and an elegant system of mimicking how the cell builds organelles like mitochondria in a test tube so that it can more easily be studied. I developed a system where mitochondria protein synthesis and import could be coupled. I was successful in conducting some interesting experiments that led to significant results, essentially supporting the concept that proteins can enter mitochondria as they are being made. In cells, protein synthesis is referred to as "translation" so the insertion of proteins into mitochondria while they are being synthesized is referred to "cotranslational protein import." That's it. That was my work.

The results I was obtaining with my cotranslational import experiments were somewhat controversial. While they were consistent with the way we believed proteins enter other cellular membranes like endoplasmic reticula, it was contrary to how we suspected proteins were imported into mitochondria, which was thought to be posttranslational – that is, a mitochondrial protein is completely made before it is targeted to and imported into mitochondria.

Some fifteen years after leaving the Schatz lab I received an unsolicited research paper from a German scientist in a competing lab in Munich. He had been working on this problem since I left the field, and claimed to have proved that I was wrong in my conclusions back in Switzerland. After reading his paper I was sure that he had overlooked something, but by that point I had no intention of returning to the bench to prove him wrong again. Even now I sometimes think it would be fun to return to the question of cotranslational protein import, but I've contented myself with simply reflecting on the friendly differences of opinion and interpretation in research science.

Jeff Schatz

At the time, I had little appreciation for the fact that Jeff Schatz allowed me to even conduct such a line of inquiry. He was clearly a posttranslational guy and much of the work from his group assumed a posttranslational mechanism. Therefore, my work actually challenged the interpretation of mechanics of mitochondrial biogenesis to which most of the Schatz lab subscribed. It was to Jeff's credit as a scientist that he actually encouraged and rewarded a budding postdoc who challenged the dogma of his field – a field in which he was clearly the world's foremost authority at the time. He could have subtlety encouraged me in other directions. He could have fired me! But instead, he put up with my irreverence toward issues presumed to be settled and permitted me to shake things up a bit. His love of scientific truth overpowered any instinct to be protective of his previous ideas and publications. In the end, whether proteins enter mitochondria cotranslationally, posttranstionally, or both, Jeff Schatz's ability to ask a question and follow results without prejudice was the most important lesson I learned from him.

When I became involved in science education after returning from Europe, I would find that the ability to question closely held beliefs using the scientific method is a skill that has no superior. Further, it is a skill, a mindset really, that must be learned. It is not natural for thoughtful humans to easily compromise their paradigms based on new observations and changing situations, yet it is crucial for intelligent people to keep from squelching new views that challenge their own. Jeff Schatz taught me this in the most effective way possible – by example.

A New Sabbatical Professor Comes to Basel

The Schatz lab, among other things, was known for the famous scientists that visited and did sabbatical research there. By midway through the second year of my postdoc, Jeff introduced us all to a new sabbatical professor who would spend nearly a year with us. His name was Efraim Racker! Not only was Racker at the Biozentrum, he and I were to be officemates. I was thrilled. I would be able to see Ef at his bench and desk daily, examining his experimental results, scratching his head, often thinking aloud.

In retrospect I think of those months as some of the best in my scientific career. At the time, however, the presence of Dr. Racker in my office added a whole new level of stress to my work. Back at Cornell I was able to talk to Dr. Racker when I wanted to, normally when I had something intelligent to say. Sharing an office with him put me under pressure to be successful and brilliant on a daily basis. This was, of course, impossible – particularly in research science. Nonetheless, I tried my best. Little by little, though, I began to realize that not all of Ef's ideas panned out either. He was wrong sometimes, and he could make mistakes. What was more, he freely admitted his errors and wrong guesses, and explained why he thought he was correct and what specifically happened to disprove his original thoughts. Therefore, he learned from everything he did, both his successes and failures. From that time forward, I was never quite so devastated by the daily mistakes one makes when trying to do something new.

Soon after Racker finished his sabbatical and went back to Cornell, Jeff and I wrote an invited review for the major American scientific journal, *Science*. The topic of the review was, of course, mitochondrial biogenesis. However, most memorable to me and I suspect Jeff as well was that we dedicated the publication to Dr. Efraim Racker, "*on the occasion of his 75th birthday*".

I would have one further meaningful and last encounter with Racker before he passed away. Within a year of setting up my own research lab as an assistant professor at The Pennsylvania State University College of Medicine in Hershey, Pennsylvania, I published the first scientific paper from my own lab. It was published with my then graduate student, Massaki Fujiki, in *The Journal of Biological Chemistry*. Soon after the journal appeared on library shelves around the world, I received a letter from Racker at Cornell. He had just read the paper. First, he congratulated me in finally making it to the scientific community on my own right. Then he pointed out that he disagreed with some of my interpretations of our published results! I could only smile.

Early Thoughts on Education While in Switzerland

While there were English speaking private schools available, we chose to send both of our children, first Keith and then eventually Emily, to Swiss public schools. Keith started in Kindergarten and went all the way through third grade. Emily only attended Kindergarten and then we moved back to the States. Following their progress through the Swiss school system, I had time to reflect on how their school experiences there differed from that in the U.S.

Swiss elementary schools were fundamentally different than U.S. schools in that a student had but a single teacher from grades one through five. In grade five, the teacher, school officials, and parents met to decide if the student should pursue a college track or begin preparing for a trade. While the actual segregation of students into these categories did not immediately occur, it was obvious that such a division was impending. I still don't know how I feel about that system.

At first blush, it seems somewhat un-American to me. The notion that such a major decision in life be taken so early, particularly with a child who has only partial say in their own future, seems harsh, even cold. However, my view is almost certainly biased by the American cultural belief that devalues the work of individuals who do not go to college. The Swiss see college much more instrumentally than do Americans. They do not believe in going to college just to decide what to do or to "find oneself". There must be a career rationale. If one is to be a writer, doctor, teacher or banker, one goes to college to become a writer, doctor, teacher or banker.

Professions that did not require college training were very well respected and often coveted in the Swiss system. This is a society in which the auto mechanics wore lab coats and the tram drivers pretty much controlled the city. Store clerks were experts in their lines. I took a broken toy back to a toy store and the clerk repaired it between customers – it was a remote control truck! Clothiers knew the differences between grades of leather and their advice was valued in making purchasing decisions. As a result, I always felt that there was generally more mutual respect amongst the citizens in Switzerland and a strong sense of pride at every level of society.

In any case, by the fifth grade, the personality traits and individual interests are developed to a point where a student more predisposed to pursuing a trade could be identified. Taking a positive viewpoint again, this gives the system more time to prepare these students for their trade and future occupation. Plus, if a student who initially headed down the trades route had a change of career heart that made a college degree essential, there was a pathway in place to make that happen as well. Therefore, the fifth grade decision was not irrevocable.

Multi-year Teachers

More interesting to me in retrospect was the concept of having the same teacher for essentially all of elementary school. This meant that a teacher, during the course of a twenty-five year career, would teach perhaps only five different classes of children. Teachers got to know each of his or her students and their families very well. Teachers would attend students' first communions and other religious and social events out of real interest in the child and family.

The Swiss system also concentrated the responsibility for a child's early learning into a single pair of hands. Since students learn to read and do core mathematics in elementary school, their one teacher had to bring each of the students up to speed. Students did not transfer from one teacher to another after only nine months. Keith's teacher was completely and solely responsible for teaching him to read German. If he could not read, there was no one to look to except Frau Jordi. The accountability was therefore enormous.

I now know that the Swiss system had two distinct advantages on a neurocognitive basis. First, since there exists a developmental standard curve for even average learners, multiyear access to students permitted teachers to help their students across grade levels. If a student was just beginning to understand an important math concept near the end of one school year, for example, the teacher could pick up exactly where she left off upon the student's return from the short summer vacation (about ten weeks). This also prevented the first several weeks of every academic year being lost as new teachers became familiar with their new students and attempted to figure out exactly where they stood developmentally and academically.

Another tremendous neurocognitive advantage of the Swiss elementary school system lies in an important component of a model of learning we will be discussing at length in later chapters – the *Information Processing Model*. At this point, let it suffice to say that we know from scientific study that whenever we encounter something new to learn, we compare it to what we already know – to our *previous knowledge* of the subject. The ability of a teacher to refer to a student's precise previous knowledge of any topic when adding to that knowledge has magnificent cognitive advantages. Following students over multiple years allows Swiss teachers to explicitly utilize a student's previous knowledge because they themselves provided the student with that previous knowledge. A new teacher can only guess at the experiences, examples, and illustrations provided by a student's former teachers, but a Swiss teacher knows. This arms the Swiss teacher with a powerful cognitive tool that only homeschool teachers can equal in the United States and in many other countries.

Frau Jordi taught Keith to read and write German. We wouldn't stay in Basel forever, though, and he would return to the U.S. school system for fourth grade. Therefore, someone had to teach him to read and write English or he would be hopelessly behind. Mary Beth accomplished this and she could tell many fascinating stories about the challenges that she faced in this daunting task. Not only did she bring him to the U.S. system exactly on grade level, but she did so for a student that was simultaneously learning to read in another language. Different vocabulary, different grammar, different sounds entirely.

Swiss Kindergarten in the 1980s

Our daughter Emily was another story entirely. She was at home with us for the most of the time we were in Basel. Only in her last year there did she begin Kindergarten. Unlike American schools at the time, Swiss Kindergartens we not located in the same buildings as the elementary schools. Basel Kindergartens were often located on residential street corners throughout the city so that they were only a short walk from a child's home. Both of our children went to small Kindergartens with only one teacher and one class. In addition, the Kindergarten curriculum was much more centered on cultural and social development than on academics. Students learned traditional songs, played games as a group, and had little pressure placed on them in Kindergarten.

Also, Basel Kindergartens could house children for a period of two years, until the child was seven and ready to go the elementary school for first grade. Thus, Swiss students began grade school (first grade) a full year older than their U.S. counterparts.

Nonetheless, by the age of seventeen or eighteen they were arguably more prepared for college than their U.S. counterparts. For example, according to 2012 PISA (Program for International Student Assessment) science literacy test results, Swiss students scored significantly higher than U.S. students. American students fared even worse compared to Swiss students in PISA mathematics literacy.

Perhaps the single greatest impact of my limited experience with Swiss public schools was simply the realization that the U.S. system of education as a whole was making a serious mistake if it thought it was the premier system in the world.

I gave a couple of lectures to undergraduate students at the University of Basel, students who had only recently graduated from high school. I, of course, had to lecture in English given my nearly nonexistent command of the German language. However, as far as the students were concerned, I could have given the same lecture in German or French and it would not have mattered to them.

By the time I left Switzerland, I was convinced that our U.S. students were going to face significant competition in the future as the economy raced toward globalization. This was the mid-1980s, a time when many of my American colleagues who did not go abroad for their postdoctoral training still lived in the comfortable dream that America outperformed other leading countries in everything, including education. From what I personally observed in Basel and through discussions with friends and colleagues from a whole host of foreign countries with whom I worked in the Schatz lab, I began to see that this was clearly only a happy illusion. Anticipating the impending international flavor of industry and commerce gave me concern of how my own children, as well as other American students, would fare in the competition. A decade later, the entire U.S. system would share my concern.

A Note About Postdocs: Temporary Paradise

I cannot leave this section without musing about the position I left in Basel. There is simply no better job, perhaps in the entire world, than being a postdoc. They are needed everywhere and can always find a job. They have few responsibilities other than following their research interests. They are called "doctor" and are respected for their scientific credentials. A postdoc can travel the world and meet fascinating people in their own language and culture. If they become bored by their area of research or fascinated by a developing research technology, they can study up and get a new postdoctoral fellowship in that field anywhere in the world. If it wasn't for the expectation that you must stop being a postdoc and become something "more" than a postdoc, either a professor, a staff scientist at a pharmacological company, or something else along these lines, and the pressure that comes with it, postdoc life would be a heaven on Earth, a scientist's nirvana.

C H A P T E R   F I V E

Assistant Professor

I RECALL THE VERY FIRST talk our entering Ph.D. class at Cornell received from its then Biochemistry Chair, Dr. Richard McCarty. He said that science in America was changing and that private corporations and other non-university entities would take a larger and larger role in employing new scientists. He admitted that the traditional track was to complete one's Ph.D. and then obtain a professorship at a university to do scientific research and train future scientists. Nonetheless, he predicted that private sector research was growing at such a rapid pace that perhaps 50% of our class of ten entering graduate students would end up in "industry."

I remember looking around the small conference room as the other nine entering students did as well, wondering who would be the five to fail to get an academic appointment when all this was over. Who would be unable to follow in the footsteps of our own professors? Who would fail to even have the opportunity to start his or her own lab, to train their own graduate students and postdocs, to be called "professor?" Which five of us would forever be consigned to "industry?"

That same question motivated me years later as I sought to exit postdoc nirvana in Switzerland and get an appointment as an Assistant Professor in America. It was not easy getting a professorship in the United States while doing a postdoc in Europe, but Jeff Schatz helped. Simply being trained in his lab was a tremendous advantage. There were many, many university departments around the world, including in the United States that would write to Jeff asking for his postdocs to apply for academic positions. Knowing that few of us had the cash to actually pay for the plane fare and lodging costs required to do job interviews in the states, Jeff even helped with the costs. The only stipulation was that we should line up a few interviews if we were going across the Atlantic, rather than planning numerous back and forth trips.

My job interview trip to the states included four stops: Harvard University Boston Eye Institute; Wayne State University College of Medicine in Detroit; Washington University College of Medicine in Saint Louis; and The Pennsylvania State University College of Medicine in Hershey, Pennsylvania. Each visit consisted of two days of interviews with professors in the departments to which I was applying and conducting a college-wide seminar about my scientific research. While the audiences at these seminars were by far the largest I had ever spoken to at the time, I found that I was not all that nervous. I ascribe this to the fact that our old Racker seminars at Cornell were so unbelievably stressful that nothing else since has compared!

Leaving Switzerland

Hershey was my last stop in the States. I felt so good about my time there that I decided to purchase a box of Hershey chocolate bars to bring back to my colleagues in the Schatz lab. At the airport in Zurich, when asked if I had anything to declare, I said that I didn't. Had they checked, I might have been the first American postdoc to get busted for smuggling chocolate into Switzerland.

The first day back at lab I got in early before the others. I left a Hershey bar on everyone's desk, from technicians and secretaries to postdocs and Jeff Schatz himself. At lunch, as much of the group gathered and chatted over their sandwiches, the Hershey bars were soon pulled out for dessert. It was interesting watching the German, French, and Swiss postdocs and graduate students take their very first bites of a Hershey bar. Everyone was polite so I have no idea what he or she really thought. However, one Swiss graduate student smacked his lips and said aloud, "I wonder how they achieve that waxy consistency." My instinct about Hershey was correct, and an offer letter arrived in the mail a couple of weeks later. We would be leaving Switzerland for Pennsylvania.

Department of Cellular and Molecular Physiology

The man who hired me was the Chair of the Molecular and Cellular Physiology department, Dr. Leonard S. Jefferson. At around that time Jim (the only name I have ever heard him referred to) was serving as the 68th President of the American Physiological Society. His lab at the College of Medicine had a long history of contributions in understanding the metabolism of liver, skeletal muscle, and the heart, with applications related to the mechanisms responsible for the hyperglycemia and muscle wasting observed in uncontrolled diabetes mellitus. Jim Jefferson was my first American scientific mentor. Tony was British/Swiss and Racker and Schatz both were Austrian.

As a new assistant professor, I was given a certain amount of "start up" money by the department. This was enough to hire a lab technician and purchase the necessary equipment and supplies to turn an empty space into a working research lab. I do not recall exactly how much money they gave me, but it was the largest sum of money I had ever been responsible for by at least an order of magnitude.

In addition, I was able to work with an architect and design my space as I wished. I had to decide where to build my office within the space; where to install the benches, gas, and water lines; how large the side rooms for new freezers, centrifuges, spectrophotometers, and other specialized equipment should be built. I needed to order everything from office supplies to radioactive isotopes. It was the most fun I have ever had in my entire life! It was like a Christmas that lasted months.

I picked items I wanted out of catalogs with the constant help of salesmen who buzzed around my door. Each day brought boxes to be opened and equipment to be set up and tested. With the passage of a couple of months my space started looking like a real laboratory, much like the one I left in Basel. I hired lab technicians to help me set up my shop and, as soon as enough of the right materials and chemicals arrived, trained them to do experiments.

There is nothing quite as satisfying as seeing the results of the first experiments performed in your own research lab. While you suspect that the laws of physics that exist elsewhere in the universe will also operate in your own laboratory, it is not until the first results are obtained that you can be sure.

The Difference Between Postdocs and Assistant Professors

What is an assistant professor? An outsider might guess that assistant professors "assist" real professors. This is incorrect except for the fact that new assistant professors often must take on some of the departmental busywork that the older professors don't really feel like doing, like interviewing prospective graduate and medical students, for example. Other than that, the main goal of an assistant professor is to succeed in no longer being an assistant professor – to become an *associate professor.*

An assistant professor does not have tenure. After a period of about five years, an assistant professor comes up for tenure review. At that time one is either granted tenure and promoted to associate professor or given about a year to find another job somewhere else.

Once my lab was set up, I was able to settle into the job of being an assistant professor. All told, the job description of an assistant professor includes performing and directing original research, publishing research findings in respected journals, writing and being awarded research grants to obtain the funds to continue to do research as well as to make a financial contribution to the department and university, teaching students, serving as an advisor to graduate students who are seeking a Ph.D. in one's lab, and performing various administrative functions such as serving on committees as assigned.

Teaching Assignments

Teaching, you may notice, falls fairly far down the list of assistant professor responsibilities. Early on we were told that tenure decisions were based on research activity (which of course included the ability to get competitive research grants), publications, and teaching, in that order. The truism that an assistant professor must "publish or perish" is based on the first two of these requirements.

So what about teaching? While the ability to teach had a stated importance and was included in one's tenure dossier, most young assistant professors understood that a poor teacher with lucrative grants and good publications would get tenure, while an excellent teacher with no grants or publications would not. It was pretty simple. Thus, the incentive to excel as a teacher of medical and graduate students was not strong.

I had two main teaching assignments beginning in my second year. The first was to deliver just a few lectures in a team-taught Human Medical Physiology course required of all first year medical students. The second was to give approximately a third of the lectures in a cross-departmental course for Ph.D. and M.D./Ph.D. students in Cell Biology. Thus my entire teaching commitment for the year entailed only about two months in the classroom giving only one lecture every other day. This is in stark contrast to some of my colleagues who ended up at undergraduate colleges and universities where they typically teach more than one class, on their own, every semester.

The Human Medical Physiology lectures, while infrequent, were the most intimidating for me as they were on blood clotting, a subject that I knew little about. Blood clotting is important, to say the very least, to a group of doctors in training. There is a whole cascade of different proteins, factors, and enzymes involved in a complex pathway that targets blood clot formation to the site of vascular injury, and it is important for students to understand how that process works. Imagine the alternative: blood clotting throughout the entire circulatory system instead of only at a site of an injury.

Eventually, though, I acclimated to teaching. At the end of each year the medical class voted for teaching awards to present to their favorite professors for their lectures. For a number of years in a row I won the "One-hit Wonder" Award, presented to a professor that the students liked but was only responsible for a few lectures.

New Approach to Science Education: Problem-Based Learning

Perhaps the earliest inkling that I was to later devote myself to the actual science of teaching came from my association with a new track offered to first year medical students called Problem-Based Learning (PBL). PBL is a student-based method of learning, removing lectures from the curriculum entirely. The PBL students were assigned to groups of about six students, each of which was headed by a professor. Each subject in the first year curriculum was approached as a problem or situation that the students had to solve as a group. Let's use an example to illustrate.

I might tell the students that a patient is brought into the emergency room with a headache, dizziness, confusion, and difficulty breathing. According to his coworkers he was near a fire containing building materials when he became ill. The question for the students becomes, "what do we need to know to resolve this situation?"

Students may ask what types of materials were being burned. They might suspect that the patient was poisoned. They can order blood tests if they know what tests to order, or x-rays. They can request results from a physical exam. Perhaps the exam leads them to suspect that the burning material emitted cyanide gas. At the end of such a discussion, in which I acted as a facilitator rather than a teacher, we would list the questions that we needed to answer to solve the problem. How, for example, does cyanide poisoning affect cells, why is it so toxic? We would then assign each student one or two of the questions, and they would be primarily responsible for providing an answer. The session then adjourned for 45 hours. Thus, we held "class" only on Mondays, Wednesdays and Fridays from 9AM until noon. Just nine hours a week.

However, between classes each student would research the group's questions. At the next meeting, we went around the table and each student would present about a five-minute overview of their assigned question. Since all of the students did some reading on every topic, this inevitably led to discussions involving increasingly detailed understanding of the topic under discussion.

While the students were initially somewhat awkward in their presentations and discussions, they became increasingly fluid in both as the semesters progressed. They learned to ask insightful and relevant questions so as not to have to research topics only marginally related to their problem. They also learned to work as a group and learned the strengths and weaknesses of each member. For example, one member might have had a good chemistry background as an undergraduate and frequently served as the group's chemistry expert. Other students became known for their familiarity with the library and could find answers very quickly in reference books. In our group sessions, when one student spoke the others would frequently be seen taking notes on what they were saying. In addition, the students were scrambled into many different groups so that each semester they had a chance to work with a number of different students as well as faculty facilitators.

The PBL approach was able to completely replace the "traditional" medical school track of attending several lectures a day, every day. The PBL students, in general, loved the alternative approach. Importantly, even though they did not attend a single lecture, the PBL students did as well as the traditional students when it came to the all important medical board exam that students had to take at the end of their second year. In other words, with no lectures whatsoever, simply by following the students' own inclinations and questions, the PBL track was able to impart essentially the same level of domain knowledge (subject matter knowledge like facts and figures) as the traditional lecture track! We felt this was an excellent result, because in addition to simply learning facts, the PBL students gained problem solving skills, communication skills, research skills, social skills, self-confidence, and other beneficial attributes.

While I was strictly a bench scientist at the time, seeing PBL's advantages I could not help but wonder to what extent an approach like PBL could be used in undergraduate education or even in K-12 education. I wondered, for example, how one could present problems of interest to young students and get them to work in small groups to solve them. My PBL experience made me certain of two educational principles. First, presentation of information outside of the traditional lecture format was much more fun for students and led to just as solid a command of domain knowledge. Second, students working in groups provided a synergistic experience that not only drastically improved learning outcomes but also taught a whole host of additional intellectual attributes. While I did not know it at the time, these two simple observations would serve as the nucleus of the LabLearner™ elementary and middle school science education system I would later design.

When I wasn't teaching, I spent my first five years at the College of Medicine doing my real job as an assistant professor: pursuing tenure. The American Cancer Society, the National Science Foundation and the American Heart Association funded my scientific research as the result of grants I had written. Four Ph.D. candidates received their degrees from my lab: Masaaki Fujiki, Jennet Beers, Samina Alam, and Christopher Kule. I published papers and lectured to both medical students in Human Medical Physiology and graduate students in Cell Biology. I did my share of committee work. Thus, when my time arrived, I was granted tenure and promoted to Associate Professor.

Next, within what in retrospect seems like a very short time, I was further promoted to full professor. The difference between associate and full professor never struck me as important as the distinction between assistant and associate professor since the latter, at least in my case, was connected to being granted tenure. Tenure is perhaps the most desired of academic achievements, as it implies a job for the rest of one's life until retirement. Becoming a full professor resulted in a small salary bump, but mainly was a title of respect, essentially stating that one had established his or herself as a leader in their area of expertise.

Thus, everything fell into place in terms of succeeding in following in the footsteps of my longtime heroes and mentors – Tony Bretscher, Efraim Racker, Jeff Schatz, and Jim Jefferson. I was one of the five students that Dr. McCarty was talking about back at Cornell when he spoke of succeeding in the "traditional track" for a scientist. Little did I know that all of this was going to rather abruptly change. Just at a point when many scientists felt they finally arrived at some semblance of career stability and permanence, I was about to embark on an entirely new venture. I would turn away from the full professorship and tenure like they never existed.

The Way Forward

PART TWO

C H A P T E R   S I X

Learning From Third Graders

MY INTRODUCTION TO THE joys and challenges of teaching K-12 science came the same way that many of us learn about the ins and outs of America's education system: parenthood.

While I worked as an assistant professor and developed my research program, our two children attended the local public school. Each year while they were in elementary school, my wife was invited to talk to our children's classes about what it was like to live in Switzerland. She took Basler Fasnacht masks and noisemakers, a crossbow, drums, flags, and a number of other items that the students could handle. Apparently she was a hit because she was asked back year after year.

The Way Forward

When our daughter Emily was in third grade, it became my turn. It was popular to have a parent come in to talk to the class about what they did for a living, and although I believed that studying how amino-terminal amino acid sequences on mitochondrial proteins targeted them to this important organelle was fascinating, my wife suggested that perhaps I should just talk about cells and bring in some materials the students could see and touch.

When the day arrived, a couple of my graduate students volunteered to help take and set up a dozen microscopes, borrowed from the histology lab, to the elementary school. On the way out of the building I dropped by the histology teaching lab and grabbed a handful of prepared human blood smear slides.

When I got to the class, my students had already distributed the microscopes around the room. My daughter Emily was happy to see me in her class. Remember, this is third grade. Most parents that go into their children's classes have made the observation that their child's joy when a parent attends their class and meets their classmates is inversely proportional to their grade level. Therefore, in third grade, while a little embarrassed, my daughter nonetheless came up and hugged me when I came in.

I began by saying that the body was made up of cells, that cells organized into tissues, tissues to organs, and so on. The students simply looked at me. I asked if there were any questions.

"When are we going to use these?" asked a student while fingering the microscope sitting in front of him. The others students then all chimed in, letting me know that they agreed that this was a good question.

"OK," I said, "do you want to see some cells?" The class came to life before my eyes and roared that they did.

"OK, but first, can someone tell me what blood is?" The answers were varied but essentially blood was in your body, maybe in veins and comes out when you get cut.

"What does blood look like?" Red and bloody, was the general consensus. With some prodding I found that all of the students knew that blood was a red liquid. One student, however, pointed out that sometimes blood was solid like a scab. This was interesting as earlier that week I had lectured first year medical students about coagulation. I simply pointed out that she was both correct and pretty smart, and moved on.

"Who wants to look at real blood in the microscope?" The class exploded into a frenzy of hand waving and discussion. I was learning!

The grad students handed out the blood smears and helped the students adjust the binocular microscopes to their small heads. One by one I heard students gasp and then smile as the blood cells came into focus. Everyone was talking to each other.

I wished to continue but it was impossible to refocus the students on me. The teacher came to my aid by clapping her hands together with a very distinctive rhythm that I would subsequently hear in a hundred different classrooms across the country: "clap, clap – clap, clap, clap." The students grew silent and the teacher signaled me to proceed.

"Does everyone see a red liquid?" I asked.

"No, no, little red dots!" the class responded.

One student raised his hand and spoke to his teacher, "Can we draw?" he asked. The teacher said yes and told the students they could take out a piece of paper and their crayons if they wished. All of the students wanted to draw.

When one observes human blood under low magnification microscopy, one observes mainly red blood cells, called erythrocytes, dispersed as simple dots on a clear background. Red crayons began tapping on desks. First a few then more, until finally every child in the class was tapping on their paper to draw the thousands of red blood cells that they observed. The sound became intense and only grew louder, accompanied by giggles, when the students realized how much noise they were making. I noticed that one student had raised his hand amidst the tapping.

"Clap, clap – clap, clap, clap." I clapped this time. The class became silent once again. I called on the student.

"Where's the blood?" he asked, "Why is it just red dots?" "The red dots must be cells." Another student shouted out.

"Yes, exactly, the red dots are called red blood cells" I said. I couldn't believe how well the students grasped the concept that all of these red dots – these red cells - together made liquid blood red. One student explained the concept to the others, if they hadn't already got it.

Another student raised her hand. "What are those blue cells?"

Most blood smears, including the slides that I had given the students, are stained with a dye called Wright's stain.

Wright's stain is often used because it stains white blood cells that are nearly impossible to see otherwise, blue.

In fact, about 95% of human blood cells are erythrocytes. Less than 1% are white blood cells. The remainder of cells are called platelets and are really more like tiny cell fragments and too small to be seen with the microscopes the children were using.

In answer to the student's question regarding the identity of the "blue" cells I said, "Good question. The blue cells are called white blood cells."

Essentially every hand in the class went up and I was stunned by how confusing what I had just said was to a group of third graders... the blue cells are white blood cells! How could I explain?

"OK," I began, "I can see how that might be confusing." I paused and thought a moment, "OK, let's not call those cells white blood cells. They have another name that maybe we should use. They are called leukocytes. The blue cells are leukocytes." That seemed to straighten things out and the students could be heard repeating the term "leukocyte" throughout the room. I felt better with the thought that I could, in fact, handle a third grader's question. My graduate students looked at me with what I hoped were expressions of respect for my ability to talk my way out of the conundrum.

As the students began to return to their microscopes to look again at these new and interesting cells, I noticed that a girl at the back of the room had her arm raised. I called on her.

"My brother has leukemia," she said, "Do these cells have anything to do with that?"

All the students stopped their individual discussions and listened. "Yeah, Megan's little brother has leukemia." "Do white blood cells make you sick?" "Does this person's blood have leukemia?" "Why do you get leukemia?" I answered as best I could, and found myself amazed at the ability of these third graders to connect my microscope lesson to the biggest concerns in their own lives.

I left my daughter's classroom energized and intrigued. Watching young students engage with the ideas and methods I used in the lab; seeing their eyes light up with the wonder of discovery as they saw cells for the first time; listening to their earnest and insightful questions about what they saw--I couldn't put my finger on exactly how, but I felt that our oft-maligned science education programs could be reformed to turn science into a passion for students.

Weeks went by, and I couldn't get thoughts of the classroom out of my head. For the first time, my brain was pushing aside questions of cells and organelles, and replacing them with a driving curiosity about children, education, and scientific learning. If those third graders were so engaged and insightful during my presentation, how was it that American students were so far behind the students I had lectured in Switzerland?

Of course, I was not the first scientist that has walked out of an elementary school classroom with thoughts flying around their head about how to improve science education, and at first I took the same approach most any of my fellow academics might take. I started looking around for reading material or a university-level course on science education to take in the evening. To this end, I visited the Penn State School of Behavioral Science and Education in Harrisburg and picked up some brochures on their Masters in Education program. However, after further thought I began to think that, to really affect change, I might want to learn more about public administration. I went back to the admissions office and picked up brochures on Penn State's Masters in Public Administration program.

I went back and forth on which new academic program I should undertake to learn about my new passion, pestering my wife with a stream of ideas and indecision about my path. Eventually she tired of my prevaricating and, seeing that if I was ever to learn about education policy I would have to experience it first hand, she took action. One day she came home and handed me a petition from the county board of elections. It had a number of signatures already. I was running for the School Board.

CHAPTER   SEVEN

School Board

HERSHEY, PENNSYLVANIA IS a small town. When I decided to run for School Board there was a population of just over 20,000. None of them knew me. It was 1992 and we had only moved from Switzerland a few years before. Add to that the fact that I was basically a scientific introvert, comfortable at my research bench but somewhat awkward under most social situations, and the chances of my being elected to public office were pretty small.

Fortunately, a couple of friends of mine, Ellen Wolpert, who was already on the School Board, and Dennis Zubler, with whom I had discussed some education-related topics regarding the same fifth-grade class our sons shared, volunteered to help me. Denny became my campaign manager. He was much better known around town than I. He owned a successful insurance agency and was very active in the local children's soccer league. He and Ellen got together a few other long-time Hershey residents to form a Committee to Elect Keith Verner and we were off.

Funds were raised, flyers printed, and hundreds of yard signs appeared around town. My neighbor Art Fasnacht and a wonderful woman who Ellen brought into the committee, Pat English, were long-time residents and consequently able to put a yard sign pretty much anywhere they felt like in Hershey, so I saw my name everywhere.

We also organized a dozen or more "coffees." These were events held in the evenings at our house or in the house of someone else on my election committee in which 20 or so people from around town were invited. There were local politicians, current school board members, professors from the medical school, teachers, and many other interested citizens. At these events, people would mull around talking to friends they hadn't seen recently, discussing their children and politics. The coffees were very friendly and informal for the most part. They did, however, require me to give a short speech.

At some point during the very first coffee, Ellen introduced me. I was very nervous. Worse, I wasn't sure what to say. I began by talking about my training, education, and so on, essentially giving no one any reason whatsoever to vote for me. At one point, someone actually asked whether I was familiar with the local schools at all, had I ever even visited one? That jogged my memory.

I began to relate the story of my recent visit to my daughter's third grade class. I could sense an immediate shift in the interest level of the group. They laughed at certain parts of the story and then fell silent when I got to the little girl's question about her brother's leukemia. I said that I couldn't understand why all of science was not taught using hands-on experiences and why the entire curriculum couldn't benefit from considering recent scientific discoveries about how the brain works. That was it. Scenes of young students wearing lab coats, using beakers and test tubes, graphing results and thinking like scientists created exciting images in my listeners' minds and spawned a communal belief that there was a way to make education better.

I was able to paint this picture time after time and from one group to another. I was amazed at how well the story did in captivating the imagination of my audiences regardless of their composition. The story of hands-on, research-based science education starting in early elementary school appealed to PTO groups, the League of Women Voters, Soccer Association parents, and business groups. The enthusiasm for the message I had found was palpable. As I told the story of how visiting my daughter's class made me, a scientist, optimistic about the future of science education, I watched audiences, made up largely of non-scientists, begin to see the issue with the same excitement that drove me into the race in the first place.

As the general election approached, I was invited to speak by local state legislators at political gatherings. I even spoke on the same stage as a US Congressman at the Harrisburg Civic Club. However, regardless of the situation, I simply related my vision. Even in the more politically focused venues, such as the League of Women Voters public debate, where issues regarding teachers' contracts, budgets and property taxes dominated, I tried to parse my answers to include logical scenarios for improving education.

It was at events like these that I developed a sense that, regardless of any other affiliation or political proclivity, people were highly affected by decisions that directly impact their children. Parents in my audiences wanted what I described for their own children. Grandparents wanted excellent education for their grandchildren. I learned that people are more similar than different. I also learned that I enjoyed talking to people more than I ever had and that perhaps I wasn't the scientific introvert I thought I was.

As I spoke time after time, the picture I painted of the way forward in education came into sharper and sharper focus. New details came to me during discussions with parents, teachers, and administrators. Ultimately, through the campaign I arrived at a clear, specific vision for science education. It was a vision that would direct my work for many years to come. In the fall, I was easily elected to the school board despite a rather crowded field of candidates.

Serving Time

Unfortunately, my vision did not prove very useful during my time as a school board member.

I began my four-year term in January of 1993. There had been several bitter divisions on the nine-person board leading into the election, related to building projects, taxes and whether to keep or dismiss the sitting Superintendent. I was voted in as a Board Officer, then later as Board President, not so much because anyone knew or liked me but because no one really knew or disliked me. In any case, I served two years as President and one year as Vice-President during my four-year term.

Early on in my tenure as a board member, I realized that for me to have an impact on the actual curriculum of the school district would take a lot of intervention and micromanaging.

This is something that I did not wish to do. I quickly learned that a school board member's job, if done well, is to facilitate the operation of the district and to approve or disapprove recommendations brought to the Board by school administration.

While I clearly stated my interest in improving the teaching of science in Hershey, I found that there was resistance to any such specific intervention by an individual board member – perhaps particularly by the President. In addition, virtually all of my and the Board's time was devoted to matters of district personnel, real estate, and litigation. During my four years on the Board, we not only built a new high school but also did major renovations on the middle school. Each year we replaced two aging buses in our fleet with two new ones. I negotiated a teacher's union contract and represented the district in a dozen minor lawsuits.

While I was not given the opportunity to affect science education in the district, my singular reason for running for office, I nonetheless learned a great deal about the American system of public education that I could not have learned as fast or as deeply by any number of university classes – hands-on learning again.

I learned about working with teachers and school administrators. I learned about teachers' contracts, their educational preparation, their professional development, their evaluation system, and the system of tenure. I learned about principal and administrator certifications. I learned about textbook approval and the ongoing cost of thousands and thousands of workbooks. I learned about school finance, school law, and the pressures of state and federal intervention on local schools. I learned about special education, gifted programs, and homeschooling. I learned about food service, transportation, building maintenance, and public relations. Maybe most significantly, I learned that education is deeply embedded in politics.

Even though I did not know it at the time, my wife's instinct to pursue practical experience was exactly right. Everything I learned in my four years on the school board would be of crucial value in my mission to improve science education in the very near future.

Classroom Lessons

More important, though, was the gradual process of understanding and articulating the things I observed on that first day in my daughter's third grade class. I wish I could say that all the lessons of that day were immediately obvious to me, but in reality it is only in retrospect, based on many years of working with children and teachers in hundreds of classrooms around the country, that I can now see just how transformational that day really was in my life and work. Many of the principles that guide our work today at LabLearner and the Cognitive Learning Institute were in play that day as well.

Importance of hands-on experience
I could have spoke to my daughter's third grade class all day about what cells are, but I doubt they would have listened very long if I did. I found myself using expressions like "Cells are the building blocks of tissue." But what does this mean when you don't know what either a cell or tissue is? Such talk often becomes hopelessly lost in analogy: "A cell is like a brick in a brick wall." Sort of, but not really. Really, a cell is like a cell. To see it is to begin to understand it.

In Emily's class, things became interesting once I stopped talking and the students began using the microscopes.

Because they could see a smear of blood on the slide with their naked eyes and then saw thousands of red dots through the lens, they concluded for themselves that the red liquid, blood, was made up of many small red dots. Now if we call the red dots "cells" they know what cells are, at least these types of cells.

Using hands-on methods also allowed the students to make their own observations. I did not tell them about different blood cell types. They saw white blood cells in their microscopes and wondered what they were. They asked and only then did I tell them. The difference between teaching by talking and teaching by touching was so obvious, I began to wonder why all of early science education wasn't done this way.

Respect children as individuals, with real individual concerns
Megan's little brother had leukemia. Nothing could be more important to her. Her special concern for her brother's blood disease led her to make a connection between two words, leukemia and leukocyte, that none of her classmates had seen.

From that moment on, I developed a keen respect for the cognitive abilities of young students. Elementary students can ask very good questions. When young learners are engaged with science that matters to them they work hard to close the understanding gap between themselves and the leading professionals in the field. In fact, it is very common to have young students ask scientific questions that not only their own teachers cannot answer, but that no living scientist can answer. That kind of curiosity is infectious, and is a huge educational asset.

The Way Forward

Teaching strategies based on cognitive science

There are "tricks" that have always worked with children and work with children everywhere. If teaching were solely an "art," governed by taste, talent, and emotion alone, it would be difficult to approach scientifically. But as the "clap, clap – clap, clap, clap" method of focusing students clearly shows, particularly by virtue of its wide-spread use, most human brains respond to certain stimuli in similar and predictable ways. The universality of many techniques utilized by teachers points to a similar conclusion. There are notable exceptions, of course. For example, I have observed that students with ADHD don't always respond as well as other students do to the hand-clapping technique. However, the exceptions can actually better inform our understanding of the rule. My early conclusion from such observations was a realization that learning, even in the complexity of a classroom, could be studied and understood.

Learning, I found, wasn't driven by random, haphazard occurrences but was governed by rules. This was important to me because if there are reproducible and predictable reactions in the learning process, there must be a scientific way to study learning.

My educator colleagues may roll their eyes at my naiveté in arriving at such conclusions. Colleges of education have taught such techniques for a century. However, had I not seen the commonalities in the human brain's response to methods and classroom practice, I would never have been interested enough to think of the matter further. For a lab scientist who suddenly finds his calling as an education reformer, these insights were the beginning of a path forward. If classroom learning could be explained from a scientific perspective, we might be able to use science to improve classroom teaching.

C H A P T E R   E I G H T

College of Medicine

THE MID-1990s SAW increased awareness of community outreach in public universities across the country. It was becoming clear that the changing economy, driven by technological advances, was going to cause American workers to switch fields a number of times throughout their lifetimes, and universities were reconsidering the mission of higher education. Continuing education would certainly play much more of a part than it had in the past as the workforce necessitated ongoing retraining. Further, with the rapid increase in online training, universities were looking to impact the population in new ways and through new mediums. Penn State University, swept up in this trend, began to speak in terms of the "engaged university," where the resources, knowledge and expertise concentrated in the traditional ivy halls of the academy were to be made available more directly for addressing social and economic issues that faced society at large.

As my frustration with the political pitfalls of impacting science education as a School Board member increased, I found an outlet for my growing passion for pre-college education in the expanding mission of the Penn State College of Medicine.

I was very fortunate in the timing of my developing interest in improving pre-college science education in American schools. Our dean of the College of Medicine at the time was Dr. C. McCollister Evarts, although most of the faculty referred to him as "Mac". He was a highly respected orthopedic surgeon and the five-volume textbook *Surgery of the Musculoskeletal System* that he edited was a major contribution to that field. More importantly, from my perspective, he saw the medical school as an important member and integral part of the surrounding community and state.

Mac was the first person to call me the morning after I won the school board election. He asked me to join the University's Government Relations Committee. Having spent my entire career a bench scientist, I initially felt somewhat awkward in a position that involved top administrators from both the College and the main University. However, my rapid acclimation to the school board eased my transition into this type of administrative task.

One day, I made an appointment to talk to Dr. Evarts to discuss an idea that I had been formulating. I wanted to start a "Committee to Support Education in Public Schools." I wanted to formally engage many of the scientific resources that we had at the College of Medicine to influence and improve education in the schools around us. Mac was immediately attracted to the concept but wanted me to present it at his next Executive Committee meeting that would be attended by the Chairs of every department in the medical school.

A week later I was waiting in the hall outside the dean's private conference room. The Executive Committee meeting was going on inside and I was waiting to be called in to present my proposal. Colleagues passed by in the hall and saw me. It was a somewhat awkward spot to wait, though I was by no means the first to occupy it. Nonetheless, I felt like a student outside the Principal's office.

The door opened and I was ushered in. There were only deans, vice presidents, and department chair people around the large table. A number of other administrators whom I had seen but never met sat on chairs along the walls.

"Keith has an idea that I think we should listen to," said Mac.

My faculty appointment was in Cellular and Molecular Physiology and my department chair, Jim Jefferson, was seated at the far side of the table. At the time he was serving as editor of the *Journal of the American Physiological Society*. He had recently overseen the committee that granted me tenure.

I went through my presentation, answered several questions and otherwise had a very nice chat with the group. I liked being there and the chairs were certainly comfortable. However, when the questions were finished it was time for me to go.

Later that afternoon, Jim Jefferson came to my office. In retrospect I think he sensed a major change in the course of my work that I had not as yet comprehended. He had hired me as a mitochondria biogenesis researcher and not a precollege science education expert, and though I didn't realize it at the time he couldn't have been thrilled by the turn in my work. I now respect how well he took it.

"How did it go?" I asked, nervous about my performance before so many administrators.

"Well, after you left the room, Mac simply said 'This kid's on fire, what do you say we help him?'" Jim replied.

Within a week I received a memo from Dean Evarts that the Executive Committee approved the committee I had proposed, made several recommendations as to its structure, and appointed me Chair. In addition, they had committed to paying a portion of my salary to the Department of Cellular and Molecular Physiology to compensate them for the time I would spend away from research. Finally, they assigned me a directorship of outreach activities and suggested that for 50% of my time I would report to the Vice-President for Administration, Charles Tandy. While I did not know it at the time, I would never publish another research paper in my original field.

Applying Neurocognitive Science to Education: The Science of Learning

Given my training and outlook, I could not possibly think about curriculum, teaching, and learning without first determining all that science had to offer on the subject. Unfortunately, most of the university-level work on the topic of education was largely relegated to the schools and colleges of education, not medical schools, neuroscience departments or other hard-science strongholds. Luckily, after I began work in my new capacity at the College of Medicine, I was assigned by the administration to a new group of multi-departmental and cross-college faculty at the main campus at State College, Pennsylvania.

By far the best thing about my new assignment was that it gave me the opportunity to drive up to main campus (about one hundred miles from Hershey) each month with the head of the School of Behavioral Science and Education at Penn State Harrisburg, Dr. Bill Henk. The long trips back and forth to State College in my Jeep were spent lost in conversation about child development, psychology, teacher training, educational psychology, and cognition. Due to the noise and rumbling of the Jeep, particularly in the summer with the windows down or the top off, Bill and I typically arrived at our meetings hoarse and thirsty.

At these meetings I got to know faculty from many different fields whose touch-points were improving the lives of children. I had the chance to hear the perspectives of Bill and others at the School of Behavioral Science and Education or my many practicing teacher and school administrator colleagues, and I learned a lot from them. But if I wanted to offer new insight I knew that I had to turn to the tools of my own trade - science. Neuroscience, radiology, and cognitive science all seemed to provide exciting avenues for increasing understanding of how learning works and how curricula might be designed to maximize learning.

Library research and discussion with colleagues immediately opened up a vast array of new experiments being done with a radiological imaging technique, fairly new at the time, called functional Magnetic Resonance Imaging or fMRI. Functional MRI is a technique allowing one to visualize brain activity with considerable resolution and in real time. Further, unlike other types of radiographic procedures, fMRI does not necessitate the use of radioactive isotopes, so it can safely be used for purely research studies. Imagine being able to have a patient read words and at the same time see exactly what parts of their brain are being used. Imagine comparing those results to fMRI imaging of brain areas that are activated when solving math computations. Hence my fascination with the potential fMRI studies could have in understanding issues in learning and memory!

Fortunately, we had some significant experts in our Radiology Department who were able to educate me in fMRI studies and run me through our MRI research facility on several occasions. Dr. Tim Mosher, Chair of Radiology at the College of Medicine today, was a resident in radiology at the time I met him and was more than happy to squeeze me into the research fMRI magnet.

One of the first studies I read using fMRI dealt with the difference between normal subjects and Attention Deficit Hyperactivity Disorder (ADHD) subjects and the effect of Ritalin treatment on ADHD brain activity. A study published a couple of years earlier, in 1998, showed much lower brain activity in several brain areas for ADHD patients versus controls. This result captivated me, given the hyperactivity of children with ADHD, I would have thought that they would have had elevated levels of brain activity, not reduced levels. Then, when children with ADHD were given Ritalin prior to imaging, normal levels of brain activity were found. This was also a striking result. Ritalin is a drug of a class called methylphenidates, which are psychostimulants. These drugs increase brain activity. Thus, the paradox of why stimulants like Ritalin should reduce hyperactivity was explained. The question of why increased brain activity should decrease the symptoms of ADHD are more complex but tell us a great deal about how normal brains focus attention and control behavior.

In short, it takes considerable brain activity to focus attention and inhibit hyperactive behavior. That's part of the reason it is difficult to concentrate when overly tired or, conversely, why one tends to become exhausted when concentrating for extended periods of time. These ADHD results opened my mind to the potential power of imaging studies in addressing other cognitive mechanisms involved in learning and memory and perhaps, I hoped, in classroom practice, curriculum design and so on.

In addition to the potential of fMRI studies, a neurophysiologist by the name of Dr. Paul Eslinger in the Department of Neurology was very helpful in getting me up to speed in some of the most up to date models of looking at learning and memory. Paul worked with hundreds of patients with various brain lesions and tumors. He was able to compare neurological and cognitive testing results with radiographic images. His understanding of human brain structure and function was therefore extraordinary. The combination of such neurological approaches with fMRI imaging studies simply fascinated me.

Chief of Developmental Pediatrics and Learning

It became clear to me that much of the scientific background, techniques and expertise that I knew I would require if I were to approach the issues of education from a scientific perspective were to be found in the clinical departments at the medical school rather than the "basic science" departments such as my primary Department of

Cellular and Molecular Physiology. I therefore spoke with the appropriate powers and, while retaining my appointment in Cell and Molecular Physiology; I became a tenured Professor of Pediatrics as well. I physically moved my office and lab to the Pediatrics department.

I was soon joined in the Pediatrics department by a new interim department chair, Dr. John Neely. Prior to becoming chair, John Neely was Chief of Pediatric Oncology and thus was an important figure in Penn States Four Diamond cancer fund and the annual Penn State student dance marathon. The "THON" is the largest student philanthropy in the world. In 2014, the THON raised over $13 million dollars for pediatric cancer research and treatment. Dr. Neely was a pleasure to work with. He thoroughly embraced the mission of bringing the totality of scientific thinking to bear on learning and teaching.

According to John, "Our patients spend much of their waking day in classrooms, how could this not be important to the child as a whole? Why should all this be outside of science and medicine?" It was John's idea that pediatricians should see themselves as members of a group of experts that study, educate, treat, and otherwise care for and about children. We should see each individual child through the eyes of all the people who support that child, and develop ways to communicate, learn, and work with each other across disciplines to help the child.

To this end, I was appointed chief of a new division; one that we were certain didn't exist in any other major medical school - the Division of Developmental Pediatrics and Learning. Most medical colleges have Divisions of Developmental Pediatrics, but we wanted to accentuate the importance of learning and cognitive functions in child development as well as the role of environments outside the clinic and examination room that had profound impacts on children's well-being and health outcomes.

In that capacity, I immediately formed a new research group called Biology of Learning and Development (BOLD). The original membership of this group was remarkable. We had the former Chair of Neuroscience and Anatomy, Dr. Rob Milner, and Paul Elsinger in the group. We had a developmental pediatrician and child psychiatrist in the group. We had Tim Mosher from Radiology and other basic science and medical researchers from relevant fields of study.

In addition to the College of Medicine faculty, I invited several experts from outside to join the BOLD group as well. My first invite, of course, was to Bill Henks, representing behavioral science and education from Penn State Harrisburg. Bill was as interested in the potential of science and medicine in teaching and learning as I. We also invited a couple of local school district superintendents to join the group. Finally, our BOLD meetings were also often attended by Drs. Jurasinski and Garner, who were first postdocs and then assistant professors in my division. This period of activity was one of the most exciting and intellectually satisfying times of my career.

Translational Research

Up to this point in my career, my research was what I would call "basic" research – the kind of research most people probably think of scientists in laboratories doing. I posed questions, formulated a hypothesis and conducted bench experiments to test the hypothesis and thus answer my questions. The kind of research that the BOLD group introduced to me is what I would call "translational" research. Instead of doing and publishing basic research in fields like neuroscience, radiology, biochemistry and so forth, we interpreted the results of such basic research in terms of teaching, learning, and memory. What does a particular fMRI study tell us about children's attention and how might that information potentially be incorporated into classroom practice or curriculum development? What do the results of cognitive testing tell us about planning the sequence of events in a lesson?

Another way of looking at translational research might be to refer to it as "applied" research. We would apply results reported by basic science and medical researchers to the problems that we tried to solve. In a sense, I suppose, we were functioning somewhat more like engineers. We were trying to take basic science research results and build something immediately useful with them. In our case, we were not attempting to build automobiles, rockets, or bridges, but rather educational programs, teacher professional development strategies, and curricula. It was totally absorbing and just plain fun.

Piecing together many aspects of basic cognitive research led us to construct an outline of the way in which information was synthesized by the brain to create permanent long-term memories. We recognized that if we were to be able to apply such a model to classroom practice, curriculum development, educational assessments, and so on, we might have considerably better control over these educational functions and perhaps improve outcomes. From the threads we were picking up across disciplines, we began to search for models to explain how learning actually takes place -- models that we hoped would be useful for gaining scientific insight into classroom learning. Models that could help guide in curriculum design and other educational applications. An example of such a model is the *Information Processing Model.*

The Information Processing Model

Humans receive and process information from the environment all the time. One of the simplest forms of information processing is the knee-jerk reflex used in basic neurological examinations. Most of us are familiar with this simple procedure. The patellar reflex is caused when a small rubber hammer is used to strike the patellar ligament located just below the kneecap (the patella). This tap causes a stretch in the quadriceps muscle above the kneecap. This stretch is sensed by a nerve cell (a neuron) that runs from the muscle to the spinal cord. This signals another neuron in the spinal cord that runs back to the quadriceps muscle and causes it to contract with the characteristic jerk of the lower leg, the knee-jerk. This processing of information is so incredibly simple that it does not even require involvement of the brain. Thus it is a very fast reflex. The brain does, in fact, become aware of the tapping--we know our knee has been tapped--but only after the knee-jerk reflex has taken place.

While the simplest form of information processing may be a reflex action like the knee-jerk, at the other end of the spectrum of complexity are learning and memory. Learning and memory may involve any or all of our senses and utilize many different areas of the brain. This is the level of processing complexity at which the Information Processing Model became useful to us.

Information processing is essential in learning and memory. In fact, if the brain does not process new information, it will not lead to permanent memories and learning will simply not occur. Conversely, the more extensively new information is processed, the better it will be remembered and the more learning will occur. The steps involved in the input and processing of new information by our brain is summarized in the illustration below.

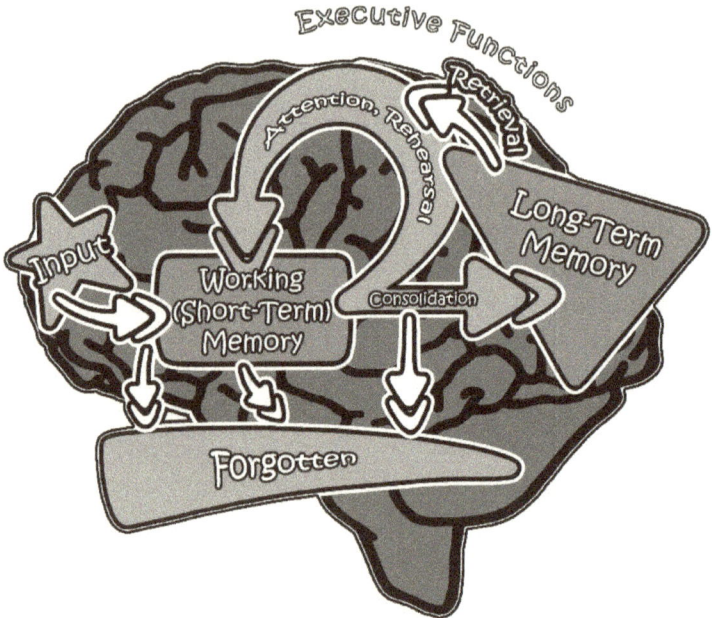

The Information Processing Model

The term **Input** at the left in the model indicates sensory information communicated to our brain through nerves connected to our organs of sensation. These sensations of course include touch, vision, hearing, smell and taste. Despite all of our cognitive complexity and our brain's ability to deeply consider the meaning of information, it is only through our five senses that we are aware of what is going on in the world around us.

At this point in our technology, there is no other way to get information from the outside world to our brain except through our five senses. Even augmented and virtual reality devices, which may soon have a significant impact on education, must deliver information through our senses to gain access to our brain for processing and interpretation. This is important to remember as we turn to technology as a mechanism to enhance learning. Not until we can somehow bypass our senses to implant stored information and the meaning of such information further downstream in the Information Processing Model, can our senses be circumvented.

In the Information Processing Model, we notice that there is a loss of information gained through input from our senses indicated by the first arrow leading downward to *Forgotten*. This indicates that some information, in fact the vast majority of information that we are presented, never makes it very far at all. We constantly receive an enormous amount of information, thousands of stimuli per second. We cannot process so much information at one time. Consider, for example, the "feel" of your right foot at this very moment. If you choose to concentrate on it, you can actually sense information being sent from your foot to your brain, its location relative to the rest of your body, for example. Obviously, it would be difficult to concentrate on anything else if we spent all of our time dealing with information coming from our right foot, let alone the rest of our body as it senses the environment. Therefore, we routinely filter out almost all information delivered through our senses. Background sounds, changing temperature, vibrations, most of what we detect in our visual fields and so on are routinely relegated to the unconscious and not processed beyond the Input step in the Information Processing Model. We filter them out and they are therefore forgotten. If we were unable to do so, the shear amount of incoming sensory information would incapacitate us.

New information that does enter the brain is available temporarily in a limited storage domain often referred to as **Working Memory** or **Short-Term Memory**, where it may either be further processed into **Long-Term Memory** or lost and forgotten (second arrow leading to "forgotten"). Incoming information from the senses is not stored long in limited storage – perhaps seconds or minutes. It is either processed or lost forever. Not only is the storage of information in limited storage brief, it is of very limited capacity. We can only place a few bits of new information into limited storage before it is filled and new information begins to replace previously stored information. It is this limited capacity of our short-term memory that causes us to so quickly forget a telephone number or street address. It is also the fleeting type of memory that causes the annoyance of forgetting what it was that we were going to look for in the kitchen after getting up from another room and walking there.

The conversion of new information from limited storage to long-term memory requires a process called **Consolidation**. Consolidation is a complex process involving comparison of new information in limited storage to "previous knowledge" through **Retrieval** of related information from long-term memory. Virtually no new information is consolidated without first comparing it to information we already have. Every bit of new information will be compared to "old" information already stored in long-term memory. Thus, if I tell you that in my living room I have a fish tank that sits just to the left of a brick fireplace and that a double French door is to the right of that fireplace, you see a version of the scene based entirely on images of fish tanks, French doors, and fireplaces that you have already stored in your long-term memory. You can't control this – all new information is encountered in terms of previous knowledge. As might be expected, this turns out to be of incredible significance in terms of teaching and learning.

Subsequent *Rehearsal* of the new information in the context of what is already known may then lead, through consolidation, to its permanent storage in long-term memory. Rehearsal comes in many forms in the classroom environment. Homework that necessitates application of information gained in class is rehearsal. One student explaining new information to another is rehearsal for both students. Students working on their lab report based on data they collected while conducting an experiment is rehearsal - and so on. Almost any time a student refers back to newly introduced information and uses it in any way they are rehearsing and it will help them consolidate the information into long-term memory.

By far, most information in limited storage never makes it to long-term memory – it is not consolidated - it is lost and forgotten (third arrow in the model leading to "forgotten"). For information to enter and remain in long-term memory, new connections between neurons in the brain must be made. This is a physical process that involves turning on genes and making proteins. Thus, learning is a physiological process that can be affected by nutrition, drugs, and the overall status of the body.

Attention and *Executive Functions* play controlling roles in the overall process. Executive Functions essentially oversee the handling of new information - it orchestrates the retrieval of relevant pre-existing information from long-term memory, guiding rehearsal while helping direct attention. Executive Functions is responsible for the integration of different brain functions. When a student decides that a new piece of information is similar to something that they have seen before, that is an example of using their Executive Functions. When a student realizes that they did not understand a concept that they just read in a textbook and decides to reread the paragraph containing it, they used Executive Functions both to check their understanding of the concept, and to formulate a plan (rereading the paragraph) for improving their understanding. Attention is required throughout information processing. No new information can be consolidated into long-term memory if we do not attend to it. Executive Functions are involved in helping students decide what they should focus their Attention on in a given circumstance. Thus, Executive Functions oversee and guide almost all areas of information processing and learning.

So Many Applications to the Classroom!

One might say that a major goal of education is to facilitate, through information processing and working memory manipulations, the accumulation of important memories in the long-term storage areas of students' brains. A second, and equally essential (although frequently overlooked) goal is to train students to access selective information from their long-term memory and to use the information to solve problems, find solutions, and create new information. As I became familiar with the Information Processing Model, I began to realize just how hands-on science instruction accomplishes both of these major goals from a cognitive perspective.

It is clear that simply "imputing" information does not necessarily lead to learning. Recall that most information never even reaches limited storage and is lost and forgotten if not processed further. Thus, "I taught them" does not mean the same as "I told them" or "I showed them." Presentation of new information to students constitutes only the first step in the process of learning. According to the Information Processing Model, "I taught them" actually means that the new information presented to the students by the teacher was processed and consolidated by the students and is permanently available to them in their long-term memory.

Eventually, after leaving the university, I would use the Information Processing Model as a guide for developing the LabLearner science program and I will return to that topic later. However, it also occurred to me that the Information Processing Model and the whole idea of thinking more scientifically about learning and memory could be of tremendous value to practicing teachers. I wanted teachers to have and understand this information so that they could use it in their own classrooms.

C H A P T E R   N I N E

Slow Starts and Lessons Learned

MY FIRST FORAYS INTO working directly with teachers and schools came as part of a larger education reform movement in the 1990s. Politicians and the press developed an interest in improving American K-12 science education during the 1990s largely as the result of US student performance on international tests such as the TIMSS (Trends in International Mathematics and Science Study) and PISA (Program for International Student Assessment). American students consistently scored lower, often significantly lower, than students in most other developed countries. These types of test results, reported widely by the media, sent out a signal that something needed to be done fast.

To make things worse, the problem of science illiteracy was not limited to American students. Every two years the

National Science Foundation conducts science literacy testing of "average American adults". The results in the 1990s were astonishing. Over half of American adults thought that lasers worked by focusing sound rather than light. Sixty-six percent did not know that the Universe began with a huge explosion. Over 50% thought that the earliest humans lived at the same time as dinosaurs (I have since referred to this as the *Fred Flintstone effect*). Only 9% could explain what a molecule is. Perhaps most shockingly, only 48% of average American adults knew that the Earth orbits around the Sun annually as opposed to monthly or weekly! Since a considerable majority of the American population had a high school diploma or its equivalent, this suggested that either they were not paying attention in class or that K-12 science classes themselves were inadequate. One way or the other, the average American adult didn't know a great deal of science.

In response to this worrying deficit in scientific literacy, many scientific institutions in the US took up the challenge to do something. One of the early leaders in this effort was Dr. Bruce Alberts, who was President of the National Academy of Science at the time. As a student, I knew Bruce Alberts as one of the authors, along with James Watson of DNA fame, of the rather thick and heavy textbook, Molecular Biology of the Cell. I had read "Cell" cover to cover more than once; it was the only textbook I carried to Switzerland for my postdoctoral fellowship and when I got there I found that it was assigned reading for all biology students at the University of Basel. In his role as President of the National Academy, Dr. Alberts attempted to impress upon the scientific community the importance of outreach work to help teachers address science education in the nation's schools. Importantly, he was also one of the driving forces behind the National Science Education Standards, published in 1996.

In response to the science literacy "emergency", many federal government scientific agencies (National Institutes of Health, National Science Foundation and many others) as well as non-governmental scientific organizations and societies took up the challenge to improve science education.

Along with every other medical school in the country, The Pennsylvania State University College of Medicine was invited to submit a proposal to the Howard Hughes Medical Institute (HHMI) for a project to improve pre-college science education. The request was sent to Dr. Evarts as the dean, who then asked me to submit a proposal.

I proposed to develop laboratories for teaching science in elementary schools in three local school districts. One was in inner city Harrisburg, another was in the Lower Dauphin School District, and the third was in Hershey. The elementary school labs were to serve two purposes. First, we would organize College of Medicine physicians and science faculty to present hands-on activities in the labs that were related to their areas of expertise. Second, we would provide elementary school teachers with a well-stocked lab that they could take their own classes to for hands-on science activities. We received the grant and while we were wildly successful in our first purpose, we were proportionately disappointed in the second.

We had many dozens of clinical and research faculty volunteer to go into our in-school laboratories. An assistant in my group coordinated the dates of the visits with the schools. During a visit, an entire grade-level of elementary students would receive instruction, rotating one class after another into the lab. We had the chair of Surgery, the vice-chair of Radiology, and faculty from departments and programs as wide-ranging as Biochemistry and Molecular

Biology, Pediatrics, Neuroscience and Anatomy, Medicine, Cardiology, Microbiology and Immunology, Physiology, and Dermatology. In addition to faculty, we had many volunteers from among the medical students, graduate students, and postdoctoral fellows. The response was quite frankly overwhelming and I was very proud to be a colleague of this tremendous group of professionals that wanted to make a mark on the community through science education.

Even as we celebrated our success in recruiting College of Medicine faculty to teach in our three local elementary school laboratories, we were dismayed at the almost total failure of our effort to encourage individual teachers to use the labs to teach their classes hands-on science. The problem was simple: without the medical school volunteers, the teachers just did not go to the labs. Never.

Even in Hershey, where I was President of the School Board, the labs went unused by the teachers. As school officials and teachers moved the lab from one room to another, much of the equipment was piled into cardboard boxes in such a manner to suggest that it would unlikely ever be used again. Worse, at one point some elementary classes were given permission to use the brand new white cotton student-size lab coats that we provided as paint smocks!

Needless to say, I was offended by the lack of respect for the materials that we provided at no cost to the school. I choose not to press the issue mainly because any intervention on my part would have been seen as a school board action rather than input from a scientist and educator. With great sadness I watched the Hershey program quickly die.

The failure of the Hershey elementary school program was a massive personal disappointment. After all, I had envisioned such a program so many times during my run for the Board. To have made it a reality and then for it to come to nothing felt like a major defeat. Nonetheless, I learned some valuable lessons from the experience that would lead to much greater success later. For one thing, materials that are provided to a school completely free of charge are not respected nearly as much as materials purchased by the same school.

To me, the interesting question was why the teachers were *not* using the labs to teach hands-on science to their own classes? There was an easy way to find out. I attended faculty meetings at the two schools where I wasn't a school board member. The teachers were very friendly and honest. They deeply appreciated the College of Medicine faculty visits and felt that their students got a lot out of the program. However, they did not use the labs with their own students for one simple reason – they didn't know how. They didn't know what they should do in the labs. They were unfamiliar with much of the equipment. They didn't know how to integrate the labs into the school district's curriculum guidelines. In an incredibly honest and straightforward way they told me that they didn't know enough about science to be comfortable teaching hands-on experiments to their students. While it was one thing to read publisher's notes and assign reading and problems from a textbook, it quite another to understand science enough to lead their students in a lab.

In my mission and passion of improving science education in the K-12 world, the input I got from the Lower Dauphin and Harrisburg teachers and administrators was the most important I have ever received. It transformed my thinking. In order to implement meaningfully improved science curricula, I would have to provide not only a curriculum that included hands on lab experiences, but I would also need to provide teachers with serious professional development. First, I needed to get them to not fear science but to enjoy it. Then, and only then, could I get them to teach hands-on science properly and with confidence to their students.

I knew I had to write a curriculum and learn a lot more about teachers and teaching. But now I had help.

The Governor's Institute for Life Science Educators

The HHMI project kept us in regular contact with many students and teachers in the public schools. Not only did we oversee the visits of College of Medicine faculty and students, but I spent considerable time in the in-school labs as well. I would observe my colleagues and do some presentations and lessons of my own. I started to develop a sense of what students at different grade levels could comprehend about science and the importance of teaching students at their level.

I also spoke to as many teachers as possible and tried to learn about the practical issues they faced in their daily routine. What did they know about science? How had they been trained at the university and what might prevent them from teaching science to their students effectively? It was a combination of these many visits to our in-school labs and what I was learning about teacher professional development as a school board member that convinced me of the importance of teacher training in ultimately accomplishing my mission of bringing excellent science education to as many children as possible.

My friend and colleague, Dr. Michael Poliakoff, was Pennsylvania's Deputy Secretary of Education for Postsecondary and Higher Education at the time. He was brilliant--a Rhodes scholar with a Yale classics degree who spoke five languages--and an extremely decent and thoughtful educator. When he and his wife adopted a beautiful little baby girl from China, Michael taught himself Chinese in a remarkably short time as well.

While not a scientist, Michael thoroughly comprehended the importance of scientific thinking in a liberal education and frequently asked me to help on various Department of Education (DOE) projects. I worked on a DOE committee that recommended the university requirements for state certification as a biology teacher. Michael also had a deep sense that many practicing teachers would benefit from serious professional development. As a result, he was instrumental in working with the Secretary of Education and Governor in creating *Governor's Institutes*--subject-directed professional development meetings for teachers across the state--in various subject domains. I was asked to organize the Governor's Institute for Life Science Educators in my capacity at the College of Medicine. Dean Evarts loved the idea and we conducted the Institute for three consecutive summers until I left Penn State.

Start In The Morgue, It Can Only Get Better

The Governor's Institutes were to be weeklong residential programs held during the summer, so the College of Medicine was a perfect place for the life science component. With the medical students gone for the summer, we had an abundance of housing available on campus. In addition, since no formal classes were held in the summer, many of the faculty colleagues I wanted to involve in the Institute would have the time to participate. The BOLD group was, of course, very much involved as well.

We limited the class size to fifty K-12 teachers from across Pennsylvania. They came mainly from public school districts but there were teachers from private and parochial schools as well. Since the demand for admission was so great, we decided to offer two one-week sessions of fifty teachers each.

I formed an advisory committee for the Institute that included teachers, superintendents and scientists in addition to an assigned DOE representative. Our students were teachers who taught elementary school, middle school, or high school. We created a schedule that started at seven in the morning and ended at seven in the evening. While there was concern in the advisory committee that this was too aggressive a schedule, it was the teacher representatives that insisted that such rigor would be embraced. They felt that most teacher professional development programs underestimated the determination that serious teachers really have. We decided to find out.

To accentuate the importance and significance we placed on the teaching of science to K-12 children and to immediately make it clear that this Institute would be different than anything they had experienced before, we decided to start the week at the morgue. I told the teachers they would begin the week with a dissection of a human cadaver and to get a good night's sleep.

Lions!

No one fainted in the morgue. Instead, the dissection exercise created a shared sense of professionalism that lasted throughout the Institute. We kept the cadaver for the rest of the week and frequently referred back to it as we discussed various other life science topics and concepts.

A couple of teachers approached me with the concern that this donor gave their body for science and that they might not have done so if they had known it would be used to educate a bunch of school teachers. At the next morning's briefing I addressed this concern and tried to describe what I saw as the stakes of K-12 science education. If this cadaver had gone the typical path, I told the assembled teachers, it would have been of educational value to a grand total of six medical students. Instead, one hundred teachers (fifty each for the two, one-week Institutes) would learn from it and then bring their knowledge to an absolute minimum of five hundred students each during their teaching careers. That would mean that this one cadaver would have contributed to the education of at least 50,000 potential scientists and doctors.

In the breakout, grade-clustered sessions, the teachers did experiments to develop lessons they could practice with their students in the coming school year. As a whole group, the teachers were able to experience experiments involving brain dissections with anatomists, neurological tests with physicians, MRI tours and discussions with radiologists, and educational technology laboratories.

One of the week's highlights was when I had a colleague from Penn State's Anthropology Department spend time with the students. Dr Alan Walker, a University of London-trained paleontologist, had recently been inducted into the Royal Society of London. He told our teachers of how the induction ceremony involved his signing a book of members that was previously signed by Sir Isaac Newton and a number of other notable scientists. We provided copies of his and his wife Pat Shipman's newly published book, The Wisdom of the Bones, to each of the teachers. The book was about Alan's work with Richard Leakey in the excavation of an African *Homo erectus* youth dating to between 1.5 and 1.6 million years old often referred to as Turkana Boy, as the fossils were found near Lake Turkana in Kenya.

In lab, Alan provided the teachers with hollow skull casts and models of early hominid ancestors ranging from *Australopithecus afarensis* through to modern *Homo sapiens*. The teachers filled the cranial cavities of each specimen with sand, transferred the sand to graduated cylinders, and estimated the volume of each individual brain. Thus, the teachers were able to plot the increase in brain size from about 400cm^3 to 1,400cm^3 during the course of human evolution.

The teachers were so impressed with Dr. Walker, that I had our team arrange an impromptu "wine and cheese" lecture that evening in the auditorium at 8PM. While strictly voluntary for our teachers, all fifty of them attended. In addition, a number of graduate and medical students attended, as well as several College of Medicine faculty that found out about the spontaneous event. I also called Michael Poliakoff, who showed up at the last minute as well.

It was a very informal session. When Alan arrived at the back of the hall where the refreshments were, he grabbed a bottle of red wine and a glass and then proceeded down the aisle to the lectern at the bottom of the hall. He had no slides and no talk planned. He would simply take any question the teachers had. This was followed by the quickest two hours of fascinating stories and discussion I can recall.

"Many scientists work in laboratories and have to deal with toxins and radioactivity," one teacher began. "What were your greatest concerns working in the field in Kenya?"

"Lions," Alan replied, setting the stage for the rest of the evening.

Among the moments that were most memorable that evening was a discussion of the evolutionary impact of bipedalism, the human trait of walking fully upright. In order to walk upright efficiently, the pelvic bones became much narrower in our human ancestors than they had been in earlier, more ape-like forms. As a result, a smooth gait that could facilitate running, jumping and other evolutionary advantageous characteristics replaced the wobbling, side-to-side, walking motion of ape-like ancestors. On the other hand, there was a disadvantage. The narrowed pelvis required to place both legs directly below the center of gravity of the human form resulted in a very small birth canal in the evolving human species. As a consequence, the size of the head at birth of our near-human ancestors needed to be much smaller to pass through the reduced pelvic bones. While ape infants are born with larger heads and more completely developed brains, bipedal infants, with their much smaller skulls have smaller and much less developed brains.

In nature, Alan explained, it is a tremendous advantage to be born with a nearly completely developed brain. Many non-human mammals are capable of walking just hours after birth. Human infants, on the other hand, are virtually helpless for an extended period of time after birth. Human infants had to be cared for and protected by the clan. They had to be taught how to survive.

This, of course, was of great interest to the teachers in the audience and speculations flew wildly regarding differential male/female specialization in evolution, development of communication, language acquisition, and so on. It was utterly fascinating and I could have easily allowed the discussion to continue all night. Nonetheless, I cut the discussion short well after 10PM and reminded the teachers that we would start up again at 7AM. By the time I got in the next morning, many of the teachers were already in the anatomy lab examining and measuring the pelvic bones of the skeletons.

All This Makes So Much Sense

Alan Walker's day at the Governor's Institute was truly a hard act to follow. We had nothing that could compete with lions! Nonetheless, it was a Thursday and the BOLD research group conducted the sessions attended by the whole Institute.

Tim Mosher discussed fMRI experiments that were beginning to tell us the functions of various brain regions. He also gave a tour of our MRI research facility and did a scan on a teacher volunteer.

In another session we discussed how, in addition to information relayed to the brain by our senses, there exists another source of information for our brains: the autonomic nervous system. This part of the nervous system feeds the brain information on the internal physiological status of our bodies and is responsive to hormones and other internal signals. Much of the information received by the brain from the autonomic nervous system is processed unconsciously, like blood pressure and blood glucose levels. On the other hand, parts of human emotional responses work through the autonomic nervous system as well. Our feelings, for example, work in part through the autonomic nervous system.

Most people have heard about or seen a lie detector test. All this test really does is record slight changes in an individual's physiological response associated with emotions. Such responses include heart and respiration rate as well as cutaneous (skin) sweating. The galvanic skin response is little more than the conduction of electrical current on the skin surface that is increased by small increases in perspiration on the fingertips. The idea is that, when you lie, your emotional autonomic response increases, as does your perspiration rate. Thus the increase in electrical conductivity of your skin is increased and detected by changes on a recorder.

We asked for a volunteer and wired up a middle school teacher. She had taught for many years and was totally captivated by the Institute. She sat at the front of the lecture hall. On one large screen we projected her galvanic skin response. On another screen next to the first, we projected a series of photographs. As the photographs we presented to her on the screen were changed, we could see her emotional response to them.

The demonstration began with a series of emotionally neutral pictures - a chair, a tennis shoe, and an empty drinking glass. Predictably, there was little response on our subject's part. Then we showed a picture of a cute baby, a flower and romantic young couple holding hands on a park bench. This elicited an obvious response from the teacher. Next, we showed a picture of a violent Nazi street scene from WWII, a news photo of a racial riot in Detroit, and the aftermath of an automobile accident. These resulted in even stronger visceral, autonomic responses. Finally, to add some levity to the demonstration, the final picture was of the US male water polo team in very scanty Speedo swimsuits. The galvanic response was immediate and large! The audience exploded in laughter, which only pushed the teacher's response further. The teacher turned red, which we explained was another autonomic response. We unhooked the subject and I told her and the audience that we played a joke and spiked the detector on the last slide on purpose. The teacher then also laughed and returned to her seat. Actually, we hadn't modified her natural response.

"Teaching Really Is Rocket Science!"

After lunch, members of the BOLD group presented the Information Processing Model to the joint session of participants. We showed imaging results and neurological and cognitive test results that led to the proposition of the various steps along the way from the input of information to the brain from the senses through to permanent storage of information in long-term memory. Paul Eslinger performed several cognitive tests on the group as a whole and directly demonstrated components of the Information Processing Model such as Short-Term Memory, Attention, Levels of Processing, and Executive Functions. Using this tag-team approach, I believe the teachers developed a fairly good understanding of the Information Processing Model.

This was confirmed when I concluded the session with an open discussion of the potential relevance of the Information Processing Model to classroom practice. To me, this single discussion was worth all the effort I had put into the Institute. The teacher's ideas poured down through the lecture hall and into my notebook. Multiple examples related to each element of the model came from teachers at every grade level. It became clear, for example, that while older children could sort through a mixture of information and decide what was important to focus their attention on for solving a problem, younger students lacked such abilities. We made up problems involving specific aspects of cognition depicted in the Information Processing Model and, by a show of hands, attempted to determine the grade level at which students developed the cognitive strategies to solve them. All of this was particularly meaningful to me because I was able to conduct the exact same discussion with a new group of K-12 teachers the following week, as well as the same Institute during next two summers. This was such valuable information.

At the end of the session I asked if there were any parting insights from the audience. One teacher raised her hand; she was a kindergarten teacher from a school in the western part of the state.

"I just wanted to say that, although I always suspected it, I now know that teaching really is rocket science!" Everyone agreed.

Questioning the University Setting

Up to this point in my life, with the exception of a few short years in Oregon, I had lived embedded within an educational system. I started grammar school, like all other American students at five years of age. After high school and college, I spent four years as a graduate student at Cornell University and then another three years as a postdoc at the University of Basel. Then I was at the College of Medicine, first as untenured assistant professor and finally as a tenured full professor. Fifteen years quickly passed as a full professor, filled with teaching, research, and writing.

The world of education was essentially all I had ever known.

But something began tugging at me to leave. At first, it was hard to put a finger on it. Part of it was that I saw the impact I was able to make outside the university on the School Board and other associated civic organizations such as the township tax association and the Harrisburg Area Community College board of delegates. Work on the university's government relations committee brought me into contact with non-university people on a routine basis. I was developing an affinity for alternative perspectives, views from outside the ivory tower. Conversely, the university perspective started to become very predictable in many respects.

My increased interaction with the "real world" outside the university, a world of business, employers, competition, profits, and taxes, showed me the complexities involved in my mission of improving science education. Although rigorous study was crucial, much more than academic discussion would be required to make an immediate impact on American education.

A New Model

As time passed, I learned more and more about teaching science to real students in real schools through our HHMI project. In addition, I developed increased confidence that I had something unique to contribute in science education. I wanted to reach more students. I wanted to have a greater effect.

The university model would typically dictate that to reach more students with our programs I would write more grants to obtain the funding to do so, and I spent a great deal of time doing just that. However, two developments dislodged me from this paradigm. First, with increased familiarity with the K-12 system of education and the development of trusted colleagues at the superintendent and principal level, I was able to discover how schools really felt about the university and university programs. This was an enlightening experience for one who knew only university life and thought that there must be no greater goal for the K-12 system than to be associated with a university!

Not so. University projects funded by grants are short lived. When grants run out, the university's involvement is over. The school, on the other hand, needs to open the next day without its university "partner." Consequently, entering into a program with a university necessitates, on the part of a responsible school administrator, a plan for continuing forward alone. This is important because it is not a question of *if* the relationship with the university will end but simply *when* it will end and what happens then.

Coupled to the short-term nature of university-funded programs is the problem that with no financial investment on the part of the school itself, without "skin in the game," schools often don't give full attention to making a program work. Teachers know the program will end, and without school financial input there is no school board oversight. If the program fails, no district money is lost. If problems develop, it is difficult to go to the board for help.

Nonetheless, it is difficult for schools to say no to the offer of free money. I recall thinking that the schools I approached had no reason whatsoever not to want to participate in our HHMI program. What would the school board say if the principal or superintendent turned down an offer for university grant funds? Wouldn't this save money for the taxpayers? It is such arrogance and ignorance that further diminishes the desirability of university programs in the minds of K-12 administrators. I was fortunate enough to overhear one of the principals in the HHMI program say straight out as I walked into a meeting, "Do we really want PSU telling us how to teach our students?" As I walked into the discussion, everyone was clearly embarrassed. I was both embarrassed and angry, although I believe I was able to hide my anger through the course of the meeting. Had I known then what I know now, I would have simply thanked the embarrassed principal for such valuable input.

The realization that K-12 schools do not necessarily accept the premise that the best solutions come from higher education was the first step on my path away from the university. The second development that caused me to rethink my affiliation with the university was quite different and involved an unusual way I found to reach more school students without obtaining grants at all.

With the help of Dr. Christine Jurasinski and others that worked in my Division of Developmental Pediatrics and Learning, I wrote up a series of experiments that could be done in an elementary school lab and organized a professional development program that taught teachers to use the lab and do the experiments with their students. While this was a very rudimentary beginning, it was, nonetheless a complete program that could help schools get more hands-on science to their students. I then calculated how much it would cost for an elementary school to purchase the equipment and supplies required to put a teaching lab in their building as well as to cover portions of the salary for those members of my group that would be involved in the process. Using Penn State's purchasing power, I was able to offer the "program" to schools for about $35,000.

Soon, school were asking, "To whom do we write the check?" A number of local school districts, learning of the program through nothing but word of mouth, were very interested. The program gave them the opportunity to deliver valuable science education experiences to students and teachers alike, and they were not obligated to the university after writing their check. They were still the owners and thus sole operators of their science program.

Around this time, there was a massive legal settlement with tobacco companies in the US. Each state received large amounts of "tobacco money" that they could spend as they wished. Some states improved their roads or made other investments. Some used the cash to pay down debt. Pennsylvania used part of its tobacco funds for health education. Since we had written up some experiments about the dangers of tobacco and alcohol, I decided to package these experiments, along with the equipment and supplies to perform them, as "Tobacco and Alcohol Kits." In one day we received an order for 67 of these kits from a single intermediate unit. Again, "To whom do we write the check?"

The answer, of course, was that the checks went to the Penn State Pediatrics department. But this was a very different kind of money. Grants contain something called "indirect costs." This is a percent tagged on to every grant written by a university to cover administrative and other overhead costs. I couldn't charge an elementary school indirect costs; it would have made no sense. Therefore, there had to be a another term for the difference in the amount of the direct costs of our products - that is, the costs of the goods sold and a certain percentage of the salary of my people involved - and the price that our schools, intermediate units, and others (let's call them customers) paid us. The businessmen and women among my readers already know the answer; it's called a *profit*! But nonprofit universities don't make profits. We were accumulating cash, but had no real structures available to reinvest that cash in program development.

Walking Away From a Tenured Professorship

It became extremely clear to me that I would be able to reach many more students and teachers if I changed my approach entirely. From my perspective, there were two significant reasons to stay at the university. One was my ability to do applied cognitive research with my BOLD group. The other was my loyalty to Dr. Evarts and my department chair, but this was soon to change.

Dr. Evarts left the College of Medicine and later the new dean brought in a new chair of Pediatrics. The replacements were excellent physicians and administrators. Nonetheless, their priorities were somewhat different and they were not involved in the startup of my work. Despite their genuine attempt to work with me, I lost much of the personal satisfaction I had in remaining at the university.

In terms of the BOLD group, I told myself that if I left the university, I would find some way to continue my research. Perhaps I'd have a department of research and development. Perhaps I'd start a private research institute. In any case, I'd find some way of doing what I would need to do to bring the very best science education I possibly could to as many students and teachers across the country as possible.

After a lifetime in academia and over fifteen years at the College of Medicine, I did the unthinkable. I walked away from a tenured full professorship and hit the road. I started a company just in time for the deepest recession since the Great Depression.

CHAPTER TEN

Starting a Company

WHEN I LEFT THE COLLEGE of Medicine, all of the people in my group left with me, including my wife Mary Beth. Mary Beth, among her many jobs in the division in Pediatrics, was an excellent grant writer. In addition, Dr. Christine Jurasinski, Joanna Garner, and Dr. Tom Freeley all went with me. Within several weeks we were joined by all of our office staff and lab assistants.

The first meeting I had with my group was at a local Red Robin restaurant. People worked from home and we continued to meet at the restaurant, once a week for a month or so, until we found a space for an office. It was on my way to one of these meetings that I got a call while in my car from Dr. Peter Bruns, Vice President for Grants and Special Programs at the Howard Hughes Medical Institute.

Howard Hughes Medical Institute

I had met Peter some years earlier. He and I were both Directors in the Howard Hughes Medical Institute Precollege Science Education Program. At that time he was a professor at Cornell University. A couple of years later Peter was recruited to HHMI to the vice president position. He left Cornell and headed to Washington, DC.

Interestingly, just prior to leaving the College of Medicine, Mary Beth, Christine, and I wrote and received another grant from HHMI to further our work in local schools. When I decided to leave the university, Christine and I drove to Washington and met with several HHMI administrators, including Peter, to tell them of our decision and to offer any help or advice they might need from us before leaving the university.

When Peter called me after I left the university, he said he wanted to discuss a proposition with me and we met soon after. The year was 2004. The Howard Hughes Medical Institute was headquartered just outside DC in Chevy Chase, Maryland. I was quite familiar with the Institute as we meet there for several days each summer with other HHMI precollege directors. It was a beautiful complex of gorgeous Georgian style red brick, white trim buildings on well-manicured grounds. The Institute had decided to build an enormous research facility in northern Virginia. It was to be located in Ashburn, Loudoun County.

According to their website, "Today, Janelia includes 50 labs and over 380 scientific researchers. In addition some 100 postdocs and 20 graduate students receive training at the facility. Each year approximately 155 visiting scientists also spend time at Janelia, representing over 25 countries from all over the world".

However, back then, there was only one pretty white farmhouse and everyone called it Janelia Farm, I believe after the family that owned the farmland previously. In 2004, the research campus was just a thick set of drawings that I could only see through the window of a locked door.

Since the Howard Hughes Medical Institute was going to become such a major new resident of the area, they wanted to be of immediate benefit to the local schools in terms of science education. In Virginia, public schools are organized on the county level. Therefore, Peter wanted to know if my new company would be interested in working with Loudoun County Public Schools (LCPS) in developing a science education program.

This, of course, would be a pleasure for me. It gave me a chance to work with Peter and HHMI. But, in addition, I was quite familiar with Odette Scovel, who was in charge of science education for LCPS. Odette attended the most recent HHMI directors meeting and we met one evening on a shuttle from the Institute to dinner at the Army Medical Museum at the Walter Reed Army Medical Center in Bethesda. It was a memorable evening. There are not many opportunities to enjoy a good dinner seated amongst one of the largest collections of medical oddities in the country. Tapeworms, one of the largest human hairballs ever surgically removed, and the bullet and skull fragments from the Lincoln assassination were on display within clear viewing distance of the dinner tables spaced among the exhibits. I recall Odette and I sipping wine and finding the hairball particularly interesting!

Loudoun County Public Schools

In our first meeting with HHMI and LCPS at Janelia Farm, we decided to develop a program for middle school teachers and students. We would develop a series of hands-on experiments for students in sixth through eighth grades and implement the very best teacher professional development programs to go along with them.

We set up a partnership between the school district, our new company - Cognitive Learning Systems (CLS) - and George Mason University. Middle school science teachers would learn about the application of neuroscience to classroom teaching, enrich their understanding of key science concepts, and implement hands-on science experiments in their classroom. We would provide 27 hands-on modules, 9 for each of the middle school grades. Part of the initiative allowed teachers to obtain graduate credits in science and education, to gain additional credits throughout the school year, and to receive continual, job-embedded professional development through classroom visits by our CLS staff who were also appointed adjunct professors at George Mason University.

Approximately two thirds of Loudoun County school district's middle school science teachers participated in the initiative and in the companion GMU graduate courses. Teachers participated for three years, each year learning new content and skills in science, neuroscience, and education.

The first requirement of the initiative involved participation in a two-week Summer Institute, led by staff scientists from CLS. Teachers discussed scientific topics including atomic and chemical structure, cellular structure and organization, genetics, mechanics, electricity, magnetism, inheritance and adaptation, and ecology. Daily sessions turned classrooms into science laboratories, where teachers conducted investigations that furthered their knowledge of these topics and became familiar with research-grade scientific equipment such as spectrophotometers and oil-immersion microscopes.

Between conversations about middle school science content were sessions in which teachers studied the cognitive neuroscience of child development, the Information Processing Model of cognition, and the neuropsychology and neurobiology of learning disabilities. The title of the initiative and graduate course was *A Neurocognitive Approach to Teaching Middle School Science.*

We had the teachers perform experiments on their own perception, learning, and memory processes, view fMRI brain scans of individuals to demonstrate how specific cognitive learning functions can be isolated within areas of the brain, and discuss how middle school students learn science during hands-on experiments. Our experience doing the Governor's Institute for Life Science Educators over the past several years provided wonderful preparation for this new venture.

After a refresher session just prior to each school year, a second component to the initiative provided teachers curriculum materials and science equipment used to conduct the classroom investigations we wrote. Teacher coaching and observation of how the investigations are taught was coupled with guidance in preparing in-depth studies of classroom and student learning processes.

This arrangement offered the highest quality teacher professional development and graduate education, and the opportunity to implement challenging, hands-on investigations that inspired middle school students to learn about all aspects of science.

While the HHMI/LCPS project was immensely time-consuming, it provided excellent professional development for very many teachers and also allowed us to develop and test over two dozen intricate sets of hands-on experiments that we designed. The project got us on our feet as a company, and around 9,000 students at LCPS directly benefited from our work.

For a five-year period, we routinely visited the teachers in their own classrooms while they performed our experiments with their students. We learned an enormous amount about science education over this period as well as making life-long friends and colleagues among the LCPS and George Mason University staffs.

Creating LabLearner

While our work on a middle school science curriculum was underway through the HHMI project with Loudoun County, we initiated an extremely aggressive push to develop an elementary school curriculum that we would call *LabLearner.*

Going into the project, I had a number of specifications that I was sure needed to be included in the program. First, based on much that I had both read and seen with my own eyes in many classrooms by that time, I knew that LabLearner would have to be nearly 100% hands-on and experiential in approach. I was not looking for some sort of add-on activity to supplement a science textbook, but rather I wanted to design a system in which hands-on experiments performed by the students themselves would be the focus of the entire curriculum.

I also knew that we would omit science textbooks entirely from the LabLearner system. In some cases, textbooks may be used effectively as supplements to real hands-on experience. I'd found, however, that many teachers who do not feel comfortable teaching science tend to use textbooks as a crutch, thereby dooming their students to only read about science and not doing it. Removing textbooks from the curriculum erased this temptation while underscoring the central importance of experiential learning in science education.

Furthermore, with the Internet offering more science content than has ever been available before, the timing was perfect for ending the reliance on textbooks. I personally would love to go back and be an elementary school student again with the Internet at my fingertips as it is now for most children in the developed world. Watching live video taken a mile beneath the surface of the Gulf of Mexico as engineers try to cap the British Petroleum oil leak at the Deepwater Horizon oil rig or watching NASA rovers turn over rocks on the surface of Mars in real time would have simply captivated me. Why, with this incredibly dynamic technology, would we want our students to lug around a silent, static, and expensive science textbook was incomprehensible to me.

So LabLearner would be 100% hands-on and use no textbook whatsoever. The next question we asked was what content should be included. We started with what we thought was a brilliantly simple plan for deciding on content: we read the best-selling science textbooks, hoping to absorb their logical progression of science instruction into our own curriculum. We found, however, that the textbooks weren't logically organized at all. Different concepts were taught at different grade levels for reasons opaque to students, and, indeed, to us. What's more, the textbooks failed to draw connections between concepts, leaving each lesson devoid of context that might give it deeper meaning. The lack of curricular organization imposed an unnecessary cognitive obstacle on students— pushing them to learn a great deal of content without the context to understand it all. This lack of specific reference to previously learned concepts, of course, was diametrically opposed to what we knew about learning from the Information Processing Model.

In terms of science content, we knew that LabLearner's hands-on approach couldn't function in the contextual vacuum inhabited by the textbooks, so we began investigating an alternative method. I invited a number of respected scientists and professionals from across the northeast to join us in Hershey to answer one simple question: what are the basic science concepts that are required to understand your field? We had representatives from each major scientific discipline, such as chemistry, biology, earth science, and physics, as well as practicing volcanologists, engineers, technologists, physicians, and other scientific professionals.

We divided our experts into groups and had them list the scientific concepts they felt were most important. The concepts were wide ranging: heat causes expansion of materials; energy is passed through ecosystems from one level of consumer to another; each atom of a chemical reaction can be found in either the products of the reaction or the original reactants; the Earth has not always looked like it does now; and so on for many, many dozens of concepts.

Next, we compared the lists and combined concepts that overlapped. We applied special weight to concepts that were relevant to multiple scientific disciplines, maintaining that such concepts are by definition "fundamental." For example, both physicists and chemists stressed what we call *conservation of matter* – that is, the law that matter is neither created nor destroyed.

After taking all of the concepts that were generated and weighting the common concepts most heavily, we finally arrive at the following grouping of nine fundamental concepts:

LabLearner Conceptual Themes

Systems
Properties of Matter
Changes and Reactions
Concentration
Force and Pressure
Force and Motion
Energy
Cycles
Structure/Function

We called these concept groupings *Conceptual Themes*. Thus, the concept of conservation of matter mentioned above would fall under *Properties of Matter*. Some concepts spanned multiple groupings. Kinetic and potential energy would, of course, fall under *Energy*. But they would also fall under *Cycles*, as in the case of the cyclic conversion of kinetic and potential energy during the swing of a pendulum. *Cycles* also includes more obvious components such as the water cycle and the cycling of rock and magma resulting in plate tectonics. *Concentration* contains concepts like the concentration of reactants in a chemical reaction, the concentration of hydrogen ions in pH, and using the concentration of molecules in a given volume to determine density. But it also contained the "concentration" of wolves that could be supported in an ecosystem containing a certain concentration of rabbits. The wolf/rabbit relationship is also found in *Systems* (as in ecosystem), as are various aspects of human physiology (circulatory system, respiratory system, etc.) and the transfer of heat between objects - the "system" being the two objects.

Lessons from the Masters

I included the above digression into the categorization of our fundamental science concepts into *themes* to illustrate a point. It is important to understand the fundamentally overlapping nature of scientific concepts. The fact that scientific concepts exist within the context of multiple disciplines suggests a logic for relating new information to information already committed to long-term memory in a multi-year curriculum. One scientific concept helps explain another. Two similar scientific concepts point to more general concepts that unite them.

Think of it this way: when we ask students to remember facts for a quiz or recall details of an experiment for a class presentation, we are asking them to imitate the masters in their field. If they excel, they remind us of an athlete who can describe every part of a play from a game long past, or of a young Mozart playing note for note a song that he heard only once before. One of the main goals of education is to build this kind of expertise, instilling knowledge in students so deeply that they can deploy it to inform any new inquiry at a moment's notice.

This affinity for recall is typical of experts of all stripes, from artists to computer programmers to scientists. The question, then, is how can we teach that sort of recall to young students? Science, educational psychology and learning theory, it turns out, provide some hints.

Scientists have long taken an interest in the question of expert recall. Originally, many questioned if it could be taught at all or if it was simply a genetically predetermined talent.

Two scientists, William Chase and Herbert Simon, conducted a study in 1973 aimed at answering this question. It involved the game of chess. A master chess player and a beginning player were shown a chessboard from a game in progress containing over twenty pieces. They were shown the chessboard for only 5 seconds before it was concealed. They were then given an empty chessboard and a full set of pieces and asked to recall as many pieces in the correct locations as possible. While the beginner could correctly recall an average of only about 4 pieces, the chess master could reproducibly recall many or all of the pieces and their placement!

Next, the researchers presented the master and beginner with boards with an identical number of pieces that were randomly placed, as opposed to presenting them with a real game in progress. Again they were shown the board for five seconds, and again were asked to recreate the setup of the pieces as best they could. The result was that the chess master and the beginner both could only remember the same small number of pieces. The master had no greater memory for chess piece placement than the beginner.

Through this and other studies, we learned that chess masters and experts in many fields have such impressive memory in their areas of expertise because they see details in terms of patterns and rules. The chess master could see a strategy unfolding in chessboards representing actual games in progress while the beginner could not. This significantly affected their ability to remember the details. The master's experience, missing in the beginner, allowed him to see meaningful relationships between the chess pieces that translated into easily remembered patterns. To the masters, context was the key to memory. The beginners had no such context.

This research should help us clarify what we're asking of our students in science class and how we can help them succeed. When we ask students to recall scientific facts - that is, to imitate science experts - we have to remember that the experts themselves didn't achieve that ability through rote memorization or genetic gift. Experts in science – scientists - organize their understanding of scientific facts around rules, laws, equations and their own experiences. Like chess masters, where others see a jumble of facts they see one or more logical systems. When presented with a new fact, they see it in terms of how the new information fits into systems they are familiar with. If a hypothetical newly discovered particle has a negative charge, the scientist understands that it must be something like other negatively charged particles. It must be attracted to positively charged particles; it must repel other negatively charged particles; it must migrate towards the cathode in a solution. Knowing very little, they can assume very much. They can attribute significant meaning to a new fact and it is consequently easy for them to remember that fact.

A student, like the chess beginner, sees only the fact, not a pattern or how the fact fits into a broader system. It is a question of pure memory work for the student, perhaps analogous to recalling a new phone number or website password.

As educators, it is our duty to develop students' understanding of scientific systems, their conceptual framework for how the universe functions. It is the business of teachers and curriculum developers to construct this framework over a course of time, making sure that each new concept builds on more basic concepts that students have previously learned. In this way, science students will develop an ability – a skill – to more quickly and efficiently incorporate new facts into an ever-growing framework of scientific understanding.

What's more, teaching science in this manner will make students more critical thinkers. If a new fact fits into a student's developing scientific framework, it can be quickly assimilated into the framework and used to sharpen a concept. On the other hand, if a new scientific fact or observation contradicts that framework, students will stop and think, saying, "That doesn't make sense." When this happens the framework must be reexamined to see how the new fact may actually make sense. In the process, not only will the new fact be learned - in a manner not at all like memorizing a new phone number or website password - but reevaluation of the entire structure of the existing framework will occur. This will lead to a deeper scientific understanding for the student. This is how the mind works. This is how science works.

In order to operationalize the lessons of research like Chase and Simon's, we made sure that LabLearner students would be exposed to the most important and fundamental scientific concepts on a repeating basis. The repetition would allow them to continually see the interrelationships between concepts and gain mastery of each one. Ultimately, we constructed the underlying fabric of the LabLearner curriculum to incorporate each of the nine *Conceptual Themes* each and every year from first through eighth grade.

The constant return to the most fundamental of scientific concepts year after year naturally led to a "spiraling" curriculum. That is a curriculum that rests on core concepts and builds complexity and depth of understanding as the years pass. Based on our knowledge of cognitive neuroscience, we were confident that the spiraling concept offered a meaningful step forward in science curricula.

Applying the Information Processing Model in Creating LabLearner

Cognitive science informed other aspects of LabLearner's development as well. A quick overview of the *Information Processing Model* immediately suggests two important roles that the classroom teacher traditionally plays in loading students' brains with essential long-term memories. The first is selecting and presenting the information to initiate the process - the *Input* step. The second is facilitating consolidation - the transfer of information into long-term memory for permanent storage and later retrieval and use.

All elements of the *Information Processing Model* were considered in the creation of the LabLearner science education system. The figure below is an annotated version of the *Information Processing Model* that points to a sample of the specific features of the LabLearner experience as they interact with particular parts of the model. For the sake of simplicity, let's take just one particular element in the annotation to demonstrate how neurocognitive considerations assisted us in the design of LabLearner.

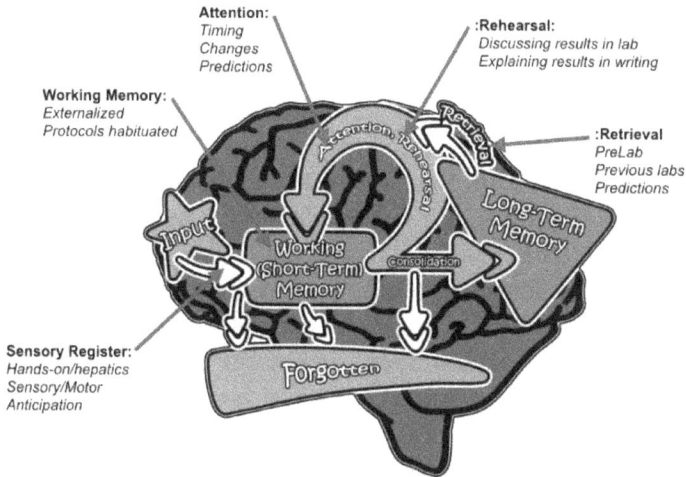

In *Working Memory*, we list "Protocols habituated." The use of the term "protocol" in experimental science suggests a stepwise method of doing something. It is something like a recipe or directions for hooking up a new appliance. The term "habituated" used in this context means to become accustomed to or familiarized with a protocol. Habituation, from "habit," often comes from repeated attempts or trials, the very repetition of which makes the protocol almost automatic, with little deep cognitive processing required. Through repeated practice, various procedures can be performed without much conscious thought. Learning to ride a bicycle, for example, requires considerable attention to detail and thought at first but once habituated, one can ride while casually observing the countryside or chatting with a companion.

Habituation of LabLearner procedures, such as using a microscope, measuring volume or calculating density, is important in the context of Working Memory in the *Information Processing Model*. As we have discussed, Working Memory is short-lived in our brains if not consolidated into Long-Term Memory. It is also very limited in size. For example, our Short-Term Memory is incapable of holding more than five or ten digits without considerable effort.

Now consider trying to learn something new in a science lab. Perhaps you are using a microscope to compare prepared slides of plant tissue and animal tissue and tasked with determining the differences and similarities between the two types of tissues. Switching back and forth between the slides, adjusting focus, optimizing light and contrast, making sketches or jotting down notes, and labeling parts creates a massive amount of new information that enters working memory. As we attempt to focus attention on what we are doing, we are also retrieving information from previously stored information about microscopes, plants, and animals from our long-term memory. The entire thought process in a comparatively simple learning task is pretty daunting when one stops to think about it!

Now imagine the same scenario with all of the aspects of microscope operation habituated. You would waste very little valuable space in working memory involving microscope procedures and protocols. You would be better able to focus on what is new. You would be better able to consolidate the new information, information related to the differences and similarities between plant and animal tissue, into long-term memory. You would be better able to learn.

Habituation is not limited to mechanical protocols. Certain thought processes can also be habituated. For example, by repeated measurements of mass and volume over the years, with subsequent application of the algorithm

$$D = m/v \quad (D\text{=density, m=mass, v=volume}),$$

one can habituate the concept of density. Thus, when a student studies atmospheric pressure, which relies on the density difference between air masses, they can focus on new concepts like barometric pressure and high and low pressure zones because the concept of density itself (air molecules per unit volume in this case) is habituated. The entire "spiraling" nature of the LabLearner curriculum works along the same lines in hundreds of cases.

A Word About Words

While we decided from the very onset that LabLearner would not use a specific textbook, we never underestimated the importance of words in learning and speaking science.

Science, like many other fields of study, has its own unique vocabulary. Scientific vocabulary, however, is inordinately loaded with concept-rich words that pose definitional challenges if students don't understand the underlying concepts. To use a common language example, consider the words *equipment* and *communism*. Let's consult Merriam-Webster:

equipment: "*the set of articles or physical resources serving to equip a person or thing*"

communism: "*a theory advocating elimination of private property*"

Both words are easily memorized. In fact, fewer words are used in the definition of communism than of equipment. Yet most would readily agree that the concept *communism* is considerably more complex than the concept *equipment*. So complex is the concept of communism, in fact, that the value of such a simple definition alone is actually quite limited.

In science, much of the key vocabulary is of similar concept-rich meaning. Let's take the term *osmosis*. Even the Merriam-Webster definition is something to be pondered:

Osmosis: *"movement of a solvent (as water) through a semipermeable membrane (as of a living cell) into a solution of higher solute concentration that tends to equalize the concentrations of solute on the two sides of the membrane"*

There may even be some issue with understanding the definition of the terms used in this definition. Let's underline the words that are likely to require further discussion in order to even understand the Webster definition of *osmosis*:

Osmosis: *"movement of a solvent (as water) through a semipermeable membrane (as of a living cell) into a solution of higher solute concentration that tends to equalize the concentrations of solute on the two sides of the membrane"*

In addition, many scientific words also have alternative common usage in the English language. This is almost always an issue when introducing young students to such words in a scientific context. For example, "I am tired, I don't have much *energy*," really can cause a problem when we wish to teach students that energy is a measurable entity that has units in joules!

The problems with teaching science through definitions actually deepen when we go from teaching scientific nouns and adjectives to scientific verbs. To illustrate the issue, let's use another common language example: *to swim*. I know the definition of the verb *swim*. I can conjugate it: I *swim*, I *swam*, and I have *swum*. However, if I fall overboard, I had better have an entirely different understanding of the word *swim*!

Similarly, learning science concepts requires hands-on experimentation. That is because many of the verbs in the vocabulary of science are, in fact, *skills*. For example, the words measure, *combine*, *equilibrate*, *determine*, *weigh*, *balance*, and *prepare* are not just scientific verbs, they are skills that we teach to science students. Defining *"spring scale"* is not the same as knowing how it works any more than knowing what a bicycle is is the same as knowing how to ride one.

The fundamental point is this: it is nearly useless to simply memorize science words! Their definitions impart very little, if any, scientific understanding. Consequently, a curriculum based on the memorization of scientific terms, concepts, and facts is similarly useless as well. A science curriculum requires a logical and spiraling sequence and abundant experimentation. Period. That is how we designed LabLearner.

Tracking progress

The key question you have to ask when you design a new curriculum is how to tell if it's working. Most curricula answer that question through standardized testing - an important but flawed metric. One of the most predictable outcomes of high-stakes standardized academic exams is that schools are strongly incentivized to teach to the test, leaving students more skilled at test taking than at science or other subjects. As we sent LabLearner out into the world, we knew that we would need a way to assess its progress that mixed standardized testing with other metrics to measure its success at not simply teaching science but encouraging scientific thinking.

Of course, we knew going in that one important metric could be easily tracked. The advantage of CLS being a for-profit company is that schools tell us every year, by budgeting money for LabLearner, that they find the system valuable enough to spend their scarce resources on it. Thus, the sheer volume and annual increases in sales tells us a lot about how schools sense the value of LabLearner and their perception that LabLearner works.

Fortunately, schools that try LabLearner are so likely to stick with it that we have long running relationships with our partner schools. When we speak with teachers and administrators at those schools about the hands-on experiments we create for their students, their input helps us understand why exactly they return to LabLearner year after year.

Given the political environment surrounding education today, standardized test scores must be a part of evaluating any curriculum. Often, schools are interested in what LabLearner can do for test scores immediately, in the first year. LabLearner students do tend to improve in the first year of the program, but as our relationships with LabLearner schools continued we found a more interesting trend: as the curriculum spirals upward, so do test scores.

As a case in point, Blessed Sacrament School in North Carolina offers a great illustration of this phenomenon. In discussions with administrators there, we learned that performance on the annual standardized science test used by Blessed Sacrament, the Iowa Test, had increased each year they had used LabLearner. Following one grade-level of students over a four-year period, science National Grade Equivalent (NGE) scores increased annually from 5.3 in fourth grade to 6.4 in fifth grade, to 8.2 in sixth grade, to 9.5 in seventh grade. The NGE data is provided to assess student educational growth over time. Results that improve with increased exposure to LabLearner are typical due to the spiraling nature of the curriculum. Why is this?

As discussed earlier, we designed LabLearner around nine fundamental scientific concepts that are revisited and expanded in the curriculum in a strategic manner from year to year. This approach makes use of students' natural cognitive tendencies to compare new information to an existing knowledge base, leading to a deeper understanding of basic concepts with the passage of time. While students almost immediately show improvement in certain aspects of science comprehension and appreciation, the spiraling nature of the curriculum promotes an ever-evolving development in science proficiency.

The fully hands-on nature of LabLearner also explains why student outcomes continue to increase with successive years of LabLearner education. They are practicing the *skills of science* each and every week in the lab! They are bound to keep getting better and better as they practice both doing and thinking as scientists. Thus, when interviewing students in LabLearner middle schools by mid-year during the first year of implementation, one of the most common student statements when asked to compare LabLearner to what they did in science the previous year is that "We did not do science last year, we just read books." Students' very notion of what science *is* matures rapidly with LabLearner.

We also found that, like a sports team on a winning streak, students that continually improve their science skills and knowledge are more enthusiastic about science. It is very common among students at LabLearner schools to have science appear as the favorite subject in end of year surveys. Some principals and superintendents have even noted that there is an issue with students coming to school sick on LabLearner lab days because they don't want to miss them.

When students are enthusiastic and teachers are delivering demonstrable results, schools often receive outside recognition for their progress. For example, nearly 20% of LabLearner schools are designated as National Blue Ribbon schools, an honor earned by only 2% of schools nationally. In addition, LabLearner schools are recognized as being among the nation's leaders in STEM programing.

STEM stands for Science, Technology, Engineering and Math. STEM schools take an integrated approach to instruction. Schools attempt to relate the STEM elements in a way that they reinforce each other and generate an overall scientific and quantitative mind-set among students.

There are other increasingly popular versions of the STEM formulation, including one that integrates art that is referred to as STEAM and a further iteration on this theme - popular among parochial schools - adds an R for religion to STEAM to create STREAM.

Blessed Sacrament has been designated as a *STEM School of Distinction* in the state of North Carolina. According to the North Carolina Department of Public Instruction, *"These schools represent the best in STEM education in North Carolina which exemplify outstanding leadership and learning that empower keen creative thinking, reasoning, and teamwork: the underpinnings of 21st century skills; in addition to implementing the essential STEM attributes needed to be successful in today's society."*

Even though Blessed Sacrament is a STREAM school, it received such distinction by the state for its STEM component alone. LabLearner serves as the base of Blessed Sacrament's STEM program.

During the process of obtaining notoriety as a STEM School of Distinction, I attended an exhibit of student STEM projects at Blessed Sacrament intended to showcase student accomplishments to state-level administrators.

We were able to speak to the students who had their STREAM projects on display. There were many interesting projects, most well advanced of their typical science fair counterparts in non-LabLearner schools. I recall in particular one project by a pair of precocious and enthusiastic students. They had designed an *app* for handheld devices that let the user view a Mars Rover crawling over whatever terrain the user chose.

I said to the two students responsible for the project, "I see the science, technology, engineering and math component of your project, but what about the Art component?"

"Who do you think did the drawings of the Rover?" they responded.

"OK," I said, "and what about the Religion component?"

There was a pause in which the two students looked back and forth at each other until finally one of them said, "Well, we prayed it would work!"

The accolades awarded to LabLearner schools tend to have a fundamental influence on the schools' overall educational community. The labs themselves become a source of pride for schools and are often visited by prospective student families, local media, and administrators and teachers from other schools. As a result, science rises in stature and perceived importance. Parents typically support LabLearner heartily and are frequently involved in fundraising efforts to implement the program. The buzz and strong reputation afforded by LabLearner only helps reinforce commitment to the program. Finally, among LabLearner's many private schools and high-end academies, LabLearner is viewed as a key component in recruiting new students.

Clearly, LabLearner works. Clearly, neuroscience and cognitive science has much to offer K-12 education in general. Putting science in students' hands and allowing them to explore their world in a logical sequence that builds their understanding generates the kind of understanding and passion for science that drove me through long nights in the lab as a research scientist. Of all the projects I've undertaken in pursuit of improved science education, LabLearner is the one that brings me the most pride and optimism for the future. It is the product of the principles I've learned from a life in science, and seeing children's eyes light up as they use those same principles to make new discoveries on their own is the best part of what I do.

Yet my interest in science education has now come to extend beyond individual classrooms. As this story arrives in the present, I find myself thinking more and more about broader questions of the future of education and the need for American educators to have a way forward to guide them into the future.

PART THREE

C H A P T E R E L E V E N

The Way Forward

Today, the LabLearner program is in schools in over half of the states in the country and is spreading every year. My son Keith is now the president of Cognitive Learning Systems, Inc., and under his leadership the company will continue to expand and improve access to excellent science education nationwide.

As for me, I am at the beginning of a new chapter in my effort to improve science education. When we created Cognitive Learning Systems to develop and distribute LabLearner, we also filed paperwork to create a non-profit called the Cognitive Learning Institute (CLI). This was because, from the very beginning, we anticipated that the creation and constant improvement of the LabLearner product would surely create worthy spin off ideas, questions, data, and innovations that would not be practical or appropriate for Cognitive Learning Systems to pursue as a for-profit organization. Getting a new business up and running was difficult enough, however, and CLI lay dormant for many years while I focused on ensuring the success of LabLearner.

I've now returned to the CLI idea as I've found myself considering education policy challenges too large to be confronted at a classroom-by-classroom level by LabLearner. There are systemic barriers to improving science education - and education broadly - that demand a long-term, focused effort to overcome. As I've stepped away from the daily operations of Cognitive Learning Systems, I've begun to build up CLI to provide just that: an independent organization that applies the values of scientific inquiry that fuel LabLearner to key questions about the long-run health of American science education.

Over years of work in the arena of education reform, I've found that questions concerning the *long run* of education policy tend to get shortchanged, to the great detriment of empirical study. I hope that CLI can be at the center of changing that trend and ensuring a future of real and continuous education innovation.

The Long Run

Imagine someone from the eighteenth century being plucked from his or her time and suddenly dropped into modern day America. They are stunned by the brightness of an athletic stadium at night. They are terrified standing near a highway where loud trucks and cars seem to be led by their bright headlights at speeds never witnessed in their century. People running down the street with cords hanging from their ears or talking loudly into their hands as if they were having a conversation would mystify them. Very little in the manmade world of today would look at all familiar and much of what they saw would be simply incomprehensible. That is, until they walked into a classroom, where children are seated at desks and tables listening to an adult at the head of the room, likely standing at a blackboard. They would conclude that they were in a schoolroom not entirely unlike those that existed in their own eighteenth century world.

Why does it seem that education has lagged so far behind other aspects of human cultural development? Certainly part of the problem is that education progresses less like the technology industry and more like the fashion industry. Fashions can change radically from year to year; there are spring colors and fall colors and then new, different spring colors. However, these sudden, rapid changes only modify superficial appearance, not deeper structure or function. There is no consistent "direction" in fashion. There is no continual "improvement". Skirt lengths go up and down and neckties shift in width and length, but skirts and neckties have remained fundamentally the same for quite some time. They are constructed of cloth fabric, thread, buttons, darts, and zippers. They function as cover for our naked bodies to a greater or lesser extent depending on "fashion." While certainly there is innovation in the fashion industry - new synthetic fabrics and Velcro fasteners are examples - our eighteenth century visitor would be neither confused or alarmed that men and women wear textiles to cover their bodies.

The technological innovations that our visitor would find so confounding, by contrast, developed differently. By and large, modern computers evolved by making gradual improvements on existing computers, much as a new biological species forms from an existing species by integrating small adaptations. We see this evolution-like development of technology even in what appear to be our most historic and radical technological innovations. The first automobiles only came about when an engine was bolted to a cart. The Wright Brothers did not start off as aircraft manufacturers. They were very good bicycle repairmen from Dayton, Ohio who dreamt of flying.

Despite the proven value of an evolutionary approach to development in technology, education innovators have often advocated frequent, radical shifts in pedagogy as though they were debuting clothing lines for a new season. We would do well to emulate examples of innovation in technology by dedicating ourselves to constantly improving an existing pedagogy in stepwise increments. By applying useful research findings and technology we may improve an existing pedagogy in a more or less predictable manner. That is, we may reasonably expect to obtain constant improvement. With consistent and repetitive application of this strategy over time, the most recent iteration of pedagogy may hardly resemble its ancestral form at all; much in the same way a laptop computer hardly resembles an adding machine or a keyboard a quill and parchment.

Science Education

The fundamental difficulty in bringing the rate of improvement and innovation in precollege science education in line with rates of advancement that are occurring in other fields is that measuring the effect of educational innovations takes time. Imagine that a *perfect* educational approach actually existed. In order to accurately observe the full benefits of this pedagogy and to experience its impact, students need to experience it from kindergarten (if not preschool) through high school graduation. This means that a time period of at least 13 years must pass simply to run one cohort through the system! Even at that point, we could only assess student knowledge and skills at the point of graduation - approximately 18 years of age. Measuring the impact of a 13-year educational program on success in college or success in a career stretches the assessment timeframe to 20 to 30 years, perhaps longer! Now consider trying to tweak the system to improve results over time. It will take a very long-term commitment indeed to substantially improve education with any degree of precision. We need to get started right away.

If long-term, well-organized techniques are essential for improving education, how capable is our current system of accommodating such approaches? Unfortunately, not at all. Typically, schools change their curriculum, staff, textbooks, and programs well before the long-term impact of an educational pedagogy can be ascertained. In addition, assessment tools and tests change as fast, or faster, than the curriculum. Academic standards come and go, often responding more to fluctuating political tides than to a clear protocol for educational improvement.

Assessments tools and teaching methods will never be universally accepted if our definition for success is not even agreed upon or thought out. Efforts to define educational success outside of the political arena today come largely from universities. However, such studies are typically funded by relatively short-term grants. Grants run out, students graduate, post-docs get jobs and move on, and long-term studies are rare. As mentioned earlier, school administrators are often very reluctant to make significant commitments to university research studies and interventions because when the projects end the administrators are left to explain to teachers and parents that their hopes for scientifically-directed education reform were dashed because a grant ran out or a Ph.D. student finished his or her thesis research.

The hodgepodge of *hit and miss* methods applied to pedagogical improvement over the past hundred years has not led to our satisfaction with the general outcome of the K-12 system. Countless hours and billions upon billions of dollars have been wasted. A much shorter and perhaps, in the long run, much less expensive approach involving a methodical, organized, long-term strategy needs to be implemented so that the next hundred years are not wasted as well. Fortunately, there is a way forward.

This will require nothing less than a fundamental paradigm shift in education. We will have to abandon the practice of frequent, major changes to the curriculum too often catalyzed by short-lived educational trends. We will instead need to adopt an academic philosophy that seeks to revolutionize education by directing methodical and continuous improvement to educational pedagogy and programs over long periods of time, on a time scale of generations, not years. This is what the Cognitive Learning Institute is positioned to do.

Cognitive Learning Institute

Cognitive Learning Institute's approach to improving science education is simple. We will study research findings in the cognitive and neurocognitive sciences and apply them to real-world curriculum development, educational technology strategies, and professional development programing and delivery. To reach as many students as possible and to assure that the benefits of our work are available to children in every socioeconomic stratum we will obtain funding to help struggling schools that could not afford to improve their educational outcomes without financial assistance.

Cognitive Learning Institute

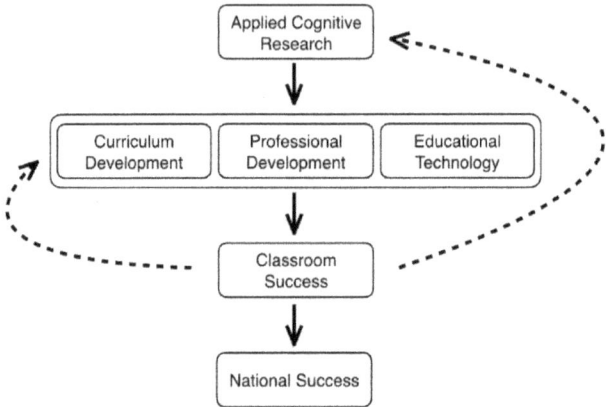

Graphically, CLI may be envisioned as in the Figure above. Applied Cognitive Research is directed at progressive upgrades in the areas indicated - *Curriculum Development, Professional Development,* and *Educational Technology.* The solid, vertical arrow pointing down from *Applied Cognitive Research* indicates this. These three applications of cognitive research are by no means the only potential applications that may develop in the future, but serve as a sampling of efforts currently underway. The second solid vertical arrow leads to *Classroom Success.* Notice there are two dashed arrows leading from *Classroom Success.* The one on the left leads back to the group of applications (*Curriculum Development*, etc.) This represents the systematic cycle of innovation, testing and improvement; the continuous pedagogical evolution aspect of the CLI mission.

The Way Forward

The dashed arrow sprouting from the right of *Classroom Success* signifies the likelihood that classroom findings will not only benefit from current cognitive research, but that classroom observations may very well suggest new areas of basic neurocognitive research. The CLI system is ideally structured to then apply such classroom-directed basic cognitive research to innovations in curriculum development and so on. This is a deeply logical and systematic system to apply, test, improve and disseminate pedagogical innovation. The system can also inform and direct future basic research to push the CLI mission even further.

The final solid arrow in the graphic shown in the Figure, the one leading from *Classroom Success* to *National Success*, represents CLI financial assistance to worthy schools that want to become part of the LabLearner network but are unable to do so. This represents both a non-negotiable commitment to fairness and an optimistic world-view that education has the fundamental power to transform society for the better and improve the lives of all children.

Cognitive Learning Institute is structured as a nonprofit organization. It is also not affiliated with any branch of government or specific government program, either federal or state. Cognitive Learning Institute is and will remain separate from government, including entities such as universities and government agencies with educational and/or scientific missions. This is because our philosophy of long-term research and development is not consistent with the rapidly changing political pressures that are constantly reshaping the mission and funding patterns of government which, in turn, have contributed to the fashion industry-like character of educational innovation for far too long. That is not to say that CLI cannot receive funding for specific studies and programs from government sources or that CLI educators and scientists may not engage in professional collaborations with government institutes or universities. Some of our employees may, in fact, hold posts as adjunct faculty in the university structure and benefit from interacting with fellow researchers in the academy.

As CLI maintains its independent and non-profit/non-governmental organizational character, it is free to determine the best strategies to accomplish its mission without excessive outside influence or pressure. The CLI board of directors consists of scientists, businesspeople, educators, and other highly accomplished individuals who are able to guide CLI into the future motivated only by a sense of commitment to children and learning.

LabLearner Science Education

LabLearner's philosophy and approach to science education is based on three simple principles. First, science education must be 100% experiential. I don't mean doing an experiment at the end of a chapter to illustrate a certain point of content. I don't mean an occasional field trip to a nature center or zoo. I don't mean a teacher at the front of the classroom performing a demonstration. I mean basing the entire curriculum, from Kindergarten on up, on laboratory experiments and discovery performed by each and every student that serve as the scaffolding on which all content is supported. I mean weekly exposure to scientific discovery and conversation resulting in hundreds of highly coordinated laboratory experiences before a student ever walks into a high school.

Second, science education must be cross-disciplinary in the sense that no divisions between the physical and biological sciences or between physics and chemistry and so forth underlie the logic of the curriculum. Science instruction should not be experienced in such silos because scientific research and discovery is not.

Finally, science education must "spiral" in increasing depth and application in both a developmental and cognitive sense along the course of an entire multi-year curriculum. Scientific concepts must be presented first at a simple level that can be easily understood by children of a particular age group. Concepts should then be made increasingly rich and detailed with advancing cognitive development over the years.

These LabLearner values are also CLI's values. We chose the LabLearner science education program because CLI staff is very familiar with the intricacies of the LabLearner program as well as its historic development. We have already seen, addressed, and solved hundreds of issues that arise in applying research-based programs to tens of thousands of students in essentially every academic environment.

The LabLearner program has proven successful over a number of years and represents what may very well be the most scholarly and thoughtful science education pedagogy currently available. LabLearner was designed entirely by synthesizing cognitive and educational research, and has been tested in diverse classrooms across the country.

Cognitive Learning Institute is able to use LabLearner's extensive database of schools, students, and teachers to test and then apply innovative new applications, closely monitoring results and making adjustments as necessary, not only guaranteeing classroom success but pushing innovations beyond anything now possible. We anticipate that ultimately CLI activities will suggest new directions in basic cognitive research that will directly contribute to improving students' success, now and into the future.

We also have the advantage of a close association with Cognitive Learning Systems, the copyright holder of the LabLearner system. Therefore, we are able to not only get fresh, up-to-date data from an incredibly large sampling of students from across the country at every grade level, but tested programmatic and pedagogical upgrades can easily be applied to the advantage of a very large number of students very quickly.

Another important advantage is that LabLearner schools have a very high degree of loyalty to the LabLearner program. They stick with LabLearner. There are exceedingly few examples of schools, having once adopted LabLearner, dropping it for another science education program or pedagogical approach. These relationships have lasted for well over a decade, far exceeding the typical curriculum cycle of any school, and are still going strong. Obviously, for CLI's philosophical approach of accomplishing long-term, systematic evolution in pedagogy, such stable interactions are perfect.

Finally, LabLearner teachers are loyal to a mission very consistent to that of CLI – LabLearner teachers are not only colleagues but also comrades and friends. They are the major spokespeople for the program and are also involved in training new teachers that enter the project. We expect that LabLearner teachers will often consult with CLI, forming its invaluable base of educator expertise well into the future.

The Way Forward

Too often, our vision for our students becomes clouded by our vision for ourselves. When we speak of creating an education system to *"prepare our students for the future,"* we are too often speaking of creating the system that we wish we could have had; one to prepare us for the realities of a world that is more connected and technologically demanding than our parents could have imagined for us. When we promise to train our students for the *"jobs of tomorrow,"* we are really referring to the jobs of today that we feel offer stability in an unstable economy because they require recently developed skills. This vision of an education system optimized for the present belies the reality that today's young people will live their lives in a future that they will largely create themselves. As we strive to give them the skills to survive in our world, we are depriving them of the skills to shape their own.

Science education is at the epicenter of this unfortunate tradeoff. Science holds the key to so many of the skills necessary to compete in today's economy that there is tremendous pressure to make sure that students learn this formula or that programming language in order to join one industry or another. Yet scientific inquiry is also a set of values at the very core of the critical thinking framework that our students will need to evaluate their world. As a scientist, I believe it is imperative that we not miss the forest for the trees in science education. Above all else, science education must give students the critical thinking tools to become better agents at improving tomorrow.

In considering our mission of preparing our students to influence the future, we must remember that today's trendy science topics will likely be replaced by new topics that we simply lack the ability to imagine today. Given that we cannot perfectly predict future scientific problems and opportunities, our best bet is to prepare our students with a good grasp of basic science facts, principles, concepts and thinking so that they can evolve along with the technology that will define their adult lives.

Put simply, it is not enough to prepare our students for the future. We must prepare them to change it.

When we set aside our vision for ourselves and examine our true hopes for the education of our students, we find something more aspirational than job training. In science, we hope that our students will be prepared to be the masters of technology. We hope they will be able to direct future innovation for the good of society. We hope they will be able to ensure that new technology and science improves the human condition and never loses sight of ideals such as fairness, justice, and compassion.

LabLearner works to realize those hopes every day by crafting and implementing science curricula for partner schools that promote scientific thought and critical thinking skills. However, reforming American science education to help our students shape the future is going to require a broader, longer-term effort. The way forward is to continue building a living and evolving Cognitive Learning Institute to stay at the cutting edge of change in cognitive science, technology, and education, so that as soon as we are able to peep around the corner into the future we have an established infrastructure for educational innovation by which we can respond.

The future will not be all bad, frightening or harsh. In fact, one would predict that along with new and perhaps awesome challenges, there would also be new and awesome opportunities. We hope that established institutional structures and, even more importantly, fluid and practical minds will be able to capitalize on nascent opportunities as they arise. As a society, we have never really taken educational innovation seriously and have never devoted undivided attention to changing the fundamental structure and paradigm of classroom practice through the application of the scientific method and cognitive research. Therefore, we have little experience in predicting the full impact of what will happen when we do. If results in other fields are any indication, however, we have good reason to be very, very optimistic.

.

www.ingramcontent.com/pod-product-compliance
Lightning Source LLC
LaVergne TN
LVHW091218080426
835509LV00009B/1059